SECRETS OF MEDITATION

SECRETS OF
MEDITATION

KIM DAVIES

IVY PRESS

First published in the UK in 2017 by
Ivy Press
Ovest House
58 West Street
Brighton
BN1 2RA
www.quartoknows.com

British Library Cataloguing-in-Publication Data
A catalogue record for this book is available from the British Library

ISBN: 978-1-78240-494-1

This book was conceived, designed and produced by
Ivy Press
Publisher: Susan Kelly
Creative Director: Michael Whitehead
Art Director: James Lawrence
Editorial Director: Tom Kitch
Consultant Editor: Richard Gilpin
Editors: Stephanie Evans, Fleur Jones
Designer: Ginny Zeal
Photographer: Neal Grundy
Illustrations: Nicky Ackland-Snow
Models: Naomi Bastable, Jonathan Cullen, Kim Davies, Alison Hahlo
Make-up Artist: Justine Rice

Printed in China

10 9 8 7 6 5 4 3 2 1

Note from the publisher

Although every effort has been made to ensure that the information presented in this book is correct, the author and publisher cannot be held responsible for any injuries or negative results that may arise.

Meditation is considered safe for healthy people. However, if you have existing mental health issues or physical problems that may affect your meditation position, then you should discuss your plan to meditate with your physician or health-care provider to make sure that it is suitable for you.

The French philosopher Blaise Pascal once said "All of humanity's problems stem from man's inability to sit quietly in a room alone."

HOW TO USE THIS BOOK This book is intended as a general guide to meditation for beginners and more experienced practitioners alike. It begins with a general chapter about developing your own practice. Subsequent chapters introduce you to a range of meditations including awareness and mindfulness practices (chapters 2 and 3), concentration exercises (chapter 4), and healing meditations (chapter 5). A final chapter explores ways to integrate meditation into your life, and looks at contemplative and other more challenging practices. You can dip into the book at any point, but it is recommended you read the first chapter before you begin your practice.

Important Notice

While the information presented within the pages of this book is useful to anyone who would like to find out more about meditation, it is important to understand that meditation practices are traditionally passed down from teacher to student. It is helpful to seek out an experienced and reputable teacher of meditation, and to practice in a class with other people. The useful addresses and websites section on page 219 provides a good starting point for this.

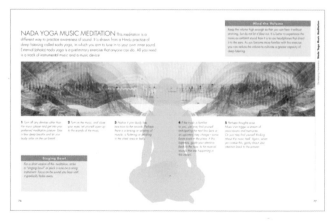

Meditation styles

Secrets of Meditation *introduces you to some of the best-known forms of meditation, from the widespread practice of focusing on your breath to the use of sacred sounds or phrases.*

Meditations

Each meditation is described through step-by-step instructions in the color pages.

Understanding

The book begins by exploring at the evolution of meditation from its most ancient roots.

Analysis

Black-and-white pages take a deeper look into the background of key exercises, and give helpful advice about enhancing your practice.

Introduction: What is Meditation?

A rich history

One of the most widespread forms of meditation derives from the ancient teachings of the Buddha, depicted here in a temple painting in Thailand.

People all over the world have practiced meditation for thousands of years. Much of the meditation we know today has its roots in either Buddhism or Hinduism, the ancient religions of India. Many people who meditate do so within one of these spiritual traditions or within one of the other great religions that have adopted meditation in one form or another—Christianity, Judaism, Islam, as well as numerous other belief systems.

However, there are many modern forms of meditation that are entirely secular. Although some of it draws on time-honored techniques, it is not attached to any theology or religious dogma. So, just as you can practice yoga without being a Hindu—or, come to that, enjoy Handel's *Messiah* without being a committed Christian—you can benefit from meditation whatever your worldview and beliefs.

This book draws on a variety of traditions. Some of the techniques have been taught more or less unchanged for thousands of years; others are relatively new and are inspired by the insights of the modern psychology movement. Some may have instant appeal, while others are challenging and require practice. You may want to focus on one meditation or you may prefer to incorporate a variety of meditative techniques into your own exploration of meditation.

There are many different styles or techniques within meditation, and these, too, are explored and explained within the pages of this book. Some of the exercises involve focusing the mind on a single thing, such as the breath, a sound, or an object—for example, a candle flame. Other methods involve the cultivation of an open awareness, in which you notice whatever is arising, moment by moment, without trying to direct your attention. All meditations are a way of regulating the mind and developing greater awareness. With sustained practice, meditation builds greater concentration, facilitates clearer thinking, and promotes emotional stability. These are just the beginning of the benefits that it can bring about. Over time, meditation can effect profound change in the way you live your life; it can alter—fundamentally and for the better—your engagement with the world. This book aims to help you along that transformational journey.

The Worldwide Traditions of Meditation

Spiritual focus
Gazing at an object is a meditative practice. This geometric design is an antique yantra, or spiritual painting, with a stylized lotus at its center.

The origin of much of the meditation we practice today can be traced back to ancient India, birthplace of Hinduism, Buddhism, and Jainism. Nobody knows how old it is, but the first written mention of meditation is in the Vedas, a body of religious writing that dates back to 1500 BCE and is the foundation text of Hinduism. Meditation itself must be much older than that first mention. It was certainly well established by the time it was cited in the Vedic texts.

Hinduism and yoga

Hindu meditation developed as a way of uniting one's inner divinity—known as *atman*—with the supreme being, Brahma. This "liberation" is called *moksha*, and is similar to the Buddhist concept of *nirvana*, or enlightenment. There are many paths toward *moksha*, and these are known as the paths of yoga. The yoga known to most people in the West is just one physical form (postures or *asanas*), but there are many others, including meditation, which is viewed as the highest path.

There are various styles of yogic meditation, many of which are concentration practices that involve focusing the mind on a particular "object." This may be an object within the body, such as the breath, or an external object, such as a candle flame. Three other popular practices are "mantra meditation," with the focus on sound; "yantra meditation," with the focus on a spiritual painting; and "deity meditation," with the focus on a god figure or its attributes.

The tantric tradition

In the West, the term "tantra" is often associated with sexual practices, but it encompasses a much wider and more subtle concept. It is an entire esoteric philosophy that is full of symbolism drawn from the Hindu pantheon, which probably developed around the first century CE. Tantric practitioners believe that spiritual realization is to be found through the senses, and tantric meditation involves the extensive use of imagery, mantras, the breath, and yoga. It is a feature of both Hindu-derived yogic meditation and Tibetan Buddhism.

Kundalini meditation is part of the tantric tradition. Its aim is to release the primal energy that lies coiled, like a serpent, at the base of everyone's spine. This force is sometimes known as the "sleeping goddess," and when it is "awakened," it is said to travel up a centered channel (or *nadi*) known as *sushumna*, opening and energizing the body's main energy centers (the *chakras*) until it reaches the crown chakra—which connects us to cosmic energy. This can be a powerful and transformative spiritual experience, so it is usually recommended that kundalini meditation is to be taught under the guidance of a reputable and experienced teacher.

Transcendental Meditation™

The Hindu guru Maharishi Mahesh Yogi brought a technique known as Transcendental Meditation™ (also known as TM™) to the West in the late 1950s. The Beatles were among his students at the height of their fame in the 1960s, and TM still draws celebrities today. It involves the use of a personal mantra, which is kept secret, and is taught only by accredited teachers. TM is widely practiced, and more than 500 studies have attested to its benefits.

Buddhism

Most of the techniques that we generally associate with meditation derive from Buddhism, and from the Buddha himself. Buddha is a title, meaning "awakened one." He was born a Hindu prince, named Gautama, in the sixth century BCE. As a grown man, he renounced his wealth so he could seek spiritual knowledge. After practicing a life of strict self-denial and meditation for six years, he embraced the "middle way"—a life of neither luxury nor poverty. He sat under a tree and spent several days reflecting and looking into the nature of his own mind. At the end of this time, he broke through the illusions of the mind and became enlightened. He understood the Four Noble Truths, which are:

- all life involves suffering
- suffering is caused by craving, whether desiring something to be here or to not be here
- the end of craving leads to the end of suffering
- craving can be ended through living an ethical life; becoming fully aware of our thoughts and actions, and developing wisdom through understanding

Buddhism focuses not on the worship of deities (or of the Buddha himself), but on his teachings, or *dharma*. After his death, these teachings were passed on by his disciples and followers, and naturally they took different forms as they spread through India and the East. Consequently, there are numerous different forms of Buddhism, each with its own unique tradition of meditation.

The different paths of Buddhism

In the centuries after the Buddha's death, his teachings were developed by various schools, of which the Theravada is the only one that still exists today. The other main strand of Buddhist teaching is Mahayana, which arose as a new vision of the Buddha's teachings.

Theravada

The Theravada tradition, which is followed in Thailand, Sri Lanka, Cambodia, Laos, and Burma, emphasizes the human nature of the Buddha and teaches that meditation and concentration are the way to enlightenment. In practice, these teachings are limited to monks and nuns. The main methods of meditation are vipassana, or insight meditation, which encourages understanding of the true nature of all things, and samatha, which makes use of single-pointed concentration, notably on the breath. These also form the basis of Mahayana meditation.

The great teacher
The Buddha asked his followers to seek the truth within themselves and not to revere him as a god. But Buddhists all over the world honor him as a teacher, and pay homage to his image.

A simple life
Theravadan monks from southeast Asia shave their heads and wear simple saffron-colored robes to symbolize their detachment from materialism.

Mahayana

Mahayana Buddhism is practiced in Tibet, China, Japan, Korea, Taiwan, and Mongolia. Compassion is central to the Mahayana tradition, and is epitomized by the bodhisattva, a being who seeks enlightenment for all beings instead of personal enlightenment. This form of Buddhism teaches that the "Buddha nature" is intrinsic in all beings, and that we can all follow the bodhisattva path in our everyday life. It also covers a diverse canon of buddhas, who embody different characteristics or aspects of the teaching. By meditating on one of these buddhas, we can help to realize these characteristics in ourselves and uncover our own Buddha nature.

Tibetan Buddhism

Tibetan Vajrayana Buddhism is a form of Mahayana Buddhism, but it incorporates elements of the tantra tradition. Its followers believe that the Buddha held back some of his highest teachings, which were discovered centuries after his death. The Tibetan tradition is rich in rituals and imagery and storytelling. When it comes to meditation, this propensity manifests itself in the use of

Sacred mountain

This shrine is high in the Himalayas. Mountains seem to be naturally conducive to meditation: They are a spectacular reminder of our own smallness within creation, and at the same time they serve as a picture of our striving toward higher things.

Turning the wheel

Prayer wheels contain a scroll inscribed with a sacred mantra. Rows of them surround Tibetan temples, and are spun by the devout as they pass.

visualizations, which are used to introduce practitioners to the experience of enlightenment. Other external aids, such as mantras (sounds) and mandalas (abstract or semi-abstract depictions), are used to guide the mind.

Zen Buddhism

The Zen tradition arose in China (where it is called *cha'an*, meaning "absorption"). It was first taught by the Indian sage Bodhidharma in about 500 CE. The main techniques used are *zazen*, or attending to the breath, and—once the mind has been steadied—*shikantaza*, or "just sitting." Under the guidance of a teacher, Zen Buddhists may also meditate on a *koan*, or impossible riddle, such as the well-known conundrum, "What is the sound of one hand clapping?"

Taoist meditation

The word "Tao" means "the Path" or "the Way," but it can also be understood as the underlying principle or the "flow" of the universe. The purpose of meditation is to achieve harmony with that deep current. Different styles of Taoist meditation are taught, some of which are similar to those used in Buddhism. Taoist meditation includes specific visualizations to cultivate the flow of chi (or energy) through the body as well as a practice called *neidan*. This complex concept is usually translated by the opaque phrase "inner alchemy," but at its simplest, it means taking care of the various aspects of one's well-being—spiritual, physical, and emotional.

Mindfulness master
The Vietnamese monk Thich Nhat Hanh helped to popularize the practice of mindfulness, which introduced Buddhism to a secular audience.

Meditation in the Judeo–Christian tradition

The Bible often speaks of meditation. The author of the forty-ninth psalm, which is part of both Jewish and Christian scripture, says: "My mouth shall speak of wisdom, and the meditation of my heart shall be of understanding." One can almost imagine the Buddha speaking those words—but in the Judeo–Christian tradition, meditation takes a somewhat different form than it does in the Eastern religions. The Christian practice of contemplative prayer, or silent reflection, in which the practitioner focuses on communion with God and on the soul, is very close in spirit to meditation as a Buddhist or a Hindu would understand it. The essence of it, after all, is stillness.

Contemporary meditation

American spiritual seekers, including Joseph Goldstein and Jack Kornfield, discovered vipassana meditation in the 1960s and 70s and brought it back to the United States. They teach "insight meditation" (vipassana). The contemporary practice of mindfulness is also derived from the vipassana tradition. It was popularized by the Vietnamese monk Thich Nhat Hanh and by scientist Jon Kabat-Zinn, who developed a therapeutic technique called mindfulness-based stress reduction. Mindfulness is a way of paying full attention to the present moment while gently accepting any feelings or thoughts that arise. It is practiced both as a formal meditation and as a way of engaging completely with any activity. It is known to reduce stress and promote feelings of calm and well-being.

A MEDITATIVE ATTITUDE

This first chapter introduces you to the benefits of meditation and shows you how to make this beautiful practice part of your daily life. It is not like other tasks or activities that are something to be mastered. The key objective is to foster attitudes of acceptance, patience, and kindness. These are the things we need to bring to our practice, as well as the discipline we need to sustain it. This chapter also looks at the common challenges faced by meditators, from beginners to advanced practitioners, and offers useful techniques for working with them. And there is practical advice on adopting a comfortable meditation posture— whether sitting, standing up, or lying down—and creating a routine that fits in with your lifestyle.

The Benefits of Meditation

Meditation is training for the mind, and its many benefits have been confirmed by contemporary research. In other words, the Western scientific method confirms the wisdom that has been taught in the East for thousands of years.

Improved focus and thinking

In meditation, we take time to reduce distractions and focus on our minds. This is an exercise in improving concentration, and is worthwhile in itself. But it has been shown that meditation improves other cognitive functions, too, such as memory and the ability to process information. Creative thinking is also aided by certain types of meditation. A Dutch study

investigated how meditation affected the ability to come up with new ideas. It discovered that those practicing open awareness meditation did much better than those who practiced only concentration meditation.

Emotional control

Meditation helps us to become more aware of our emotions and release their grip on us. This can help us to handle stress and conflict. Specific practices, such as the loving-kindness meditation (see page 138), have been shown to increase empathy and willingness to help others. One study has shown that practicing mindfulness meditation for eight weeks—the length of the mindfulness-based stress reduction course developed by Jon Kabat-Zinn—reduced gray matter in the amygdala, the part of the brain connected to fear and stress. Regular meditation can instill a deep sense of gratitude for life, creating greater happiness.

Safe Meditation

Meditation is considered safe for healthy people. However, if you have existing mental health issues or physical problems that may affect your meditation position, then you should discuss your plan to meditate with your physician or health-care provider to make sure that it is suitable for you.

Meditation and health

Meditation is good for the body as well as the mind. It can strengthen the immune system, lower blood pressure and the heart rate, and even help you deal with pain. One study of patients with coronary heart disease assigned its 201 participants either a Transcendental Meditation™ or a health-education class. The meditators had a 48 percent lower risk of heart attack, stroke, or death in the five years following the study.

EXPLORING YOUR MOTIVATION
Meditation is about exploration, so it can be counterproductive to have a particular goal or outcome in mind. All the same, it is worth spending some time thinking about the reasons you want to try meditation, because this may help your motivation and can also affect the kind of meditation that you choose to do. Try this exploratory exercise.

1 *Find some paper and a pen so that you can write notes.*

2 *Sit comfortably in a quiet place where you won't be disturbed. Take a deep breath in and out— you may want to release a loud sigh as you do this. Spend a few moments sitting and breathing, with your eyes closed.*

3 *Ask yourself the following questions:*
Why do I want to practice meditation?
What has led me to trying meditation?
What am I hoping to gain from meditation?
What do I expect to happen?

4 Sometimes the answer may be specific—for example to feel less stressed. Or it may be simply that someone has suggested that you should try it. Perhaps you feel it will improve your performance at work, or that it will help you with anxiety or a particular health issue. Whatever comes to mind, write it down on the paper without judging your thoughts and feelings.

5 Continue to sit, breathing naturally. Does anything else come to mind? Don't worry if your motivation is only to see what happens (that's great), or to reach a seemingly impossible goal (such as to understand the meaning of life, which is also great). All you are doing here is beginning a process of exploration that is part of meditation practice.

6 Put your notes somewhere safe. It can be useful to refer to these later and explore whether your expectations and underlying motivations have changed with practice.

Developing the Right Attitude

Meditation can too easily become a chore. Or we can develop the false idea that it should be effortless, and then get discouraged when it is nothing of the kind. There are many unhelpful ways of approaching meditation. Here are some elements of the right attitude to bring to your practice.

Patience and curiosity

Meditation is a process of watching. If you are impatient for something to happen or to stop happening, it will block you from experiencing what *is* happening. So cultivate an attitude of patience, because this allows you to return to your focus again and again. Patience should go alongside curiosity and being interested in your experience. This enables you to be ready to receive and know the wealth of possibilities that lie in each moment.

Acceptance

In meditation, we acknowledge our experience in the here and now, instead of trying to control, change, or take mental flight from it. This is the attitude of acceptance. It means acknowledging the reality of a situation. Acceptance is not the same as endurance or apathy. We can still choose to change our experience if that is necessary and possible, but we do so with awareness instead of reacting blindly, feeling powerless, or gritting our teeth.

Kindness

In meditation, we are kind to ourselves. We do not berate ourselves for our failures; instead, we acknowledge them and gently bring ourselves back to our chosen path or method. Kindness is not, however, the same as laziness or apathy. Meditation requires us to engage with commitment and alertness, instead of sitting back passively.

Releasing expectation

Try to let go of any sense of goals when you are ready to meditate. You cannot know what the results of a particular or sustained practice will be, so feeling that a particular meditation was "good" or "bad" is an illusion. When you are ready to meditate, let go of your desire for it to achieve something or take you somewhere.

Tuning Up

The Buddha compared the effort to train the mind to a musical instrument on which the strings must be tightened to exactly the right degree. When we practice, our focus must be properly tuned; if we tense up too much, or if our attention is too slack, we will not be able to resonate with the moment.

BUILDING A REGULAR PRACTICE

One useful way to build a meditation practice is to have a regular time and place when we come to sit on our cushion or chair. Here are some ways to help integrate meditation into your daily life.

1 Make a commitment

Decide how often you want to meditate—say, twice a week for five minutes—and write that goal down. Or put your meditation time on your calendar with any other appointments.

2 Set small goals

Being overambitious can be counterproductive. So start with an achievable aim, such as meditating for five minutes a day.

3 Increase slowly

When you achieve your goal of sitting twice a week for several weeks, increase it to three times a week.

Practice with Others

Many people find it easier to meditate in a class, where they draw on the motivation of others and take inspiration from a teacher. It is important to choose a knowledgeable teacher who sustains a regular practice and has the wisdom to guide others. The easiest way to find a teacher is through a reputable organization; there is a list in the back of the book.

4 Use reminders

Set an alert to remind you it is time to practice (choose a pleasurable sound, such as a chime). Or link your meditation practice to some well-established habit. For example, if you always change your clothes when you come home from work, make this the time you meditate.

5 Celebrate your achievement

Acknowledge that it is an achievement to fit meditation into a busy life and to have the self-discipline to stick with it. Congratulate yourself every time you meditate.

6 Don't judge it

Sometimes meditation feels pleasurable, even blissful; at others, we find ourselves distracted or sleepy throughout much of our practice. If you find yourself thinking you have had a bad or good practice, be aware that this is judging and let it go. Accepting your experience for what it is makes it easier to persevere with your practice.

Common Obstacles

Ancient Buddhist sources speak of the "five hindrances" or obstacles to practice. These are restlessness, sloth and torpor (sleepiness), aversion and ill will, sensual desire, and doubt. Throughout history, every meditator has faced them. The RAIN technique, which you will find on pages 30–31, is a useful tool in dealing with these obstacles to practice, and there are many other simple techniques you can try.

Restlessness

If you regularly feel fidgety or restless when you sit, try walking meditation (see pages 94–97), or practice after physical activity. It helps to create a small goal, such as focusing for five breaths, or to give your mind more to do by broadening your awareness, perhaps to sound. Feeling unable to settle can be a form of avoidance—if you investigate your restlessness, you may discover an uncomfortable emotion lies beneath.

Sleepiness

If you feel sleepy or sluggish during meditation, you can bring more energy to the body by keeping an erect posture, standing up, taking deep breaths, or gently massaging the earlobes. Give the mind something specific to do, such as silently labeling the in breath and the out breath (see pages 56–57) or counting your breaths (see pages 60–61). Sometimes drowsiness is a sign that you do, in fact, need to make more time for sleep.

Aversion and ill will

When we meditate, we may find some aspect of our experience or environment displeasing. Our natural inclination is to push unpleasant feelings or experiences away; this is aversion, and it can intensify into stronger feelings of ill will. Changing your focus—either broadening or narrowing it—can be helpful to deal with aversion or ill will, and it is also useful to think of cradling an unpleasant emotion or feeling like a mother cradles a baby. Goodwill practices, such as loving-kindness (see page 138), can be a helpful counterbalance.

Sensual desire

Sitting on the mat, you may find yourself caught up in dreamy thoughts and fantasies about food, sex, cigarettes,

or something similar. The best way to deal with these thoughts is to examine them, using the RAIN technique. But for persistent cravings, try reflecting on their temporary nature—even when they are satisfied they soon recur—or on the less appealing side of the thing we are craving (for example, the harmful effects of a cigarette, or the bodily functions of the person we are fantasizing about).

Doubt

It is common to question the reasons for meditation, or to feel that it won't work for you. Some people find it helpful to research the attested benefits of meditation, or to seek out an experienced teacher to discuss those doubts. Once you are on your cushion or chair, label your doubts "thinking" — and then let them go.

THE RAIN TECHNIQUE

When we face difficulty, our usual attitude is to try to wish it away. But leaning into it, welcoming it as a worthy object of investigation, can change our attitude toward difficulty, and—paradoxically—this may sometimes be all that is needed to make a trouble dissipate. So our first response to a challenge in

1 Recognition

Notice what is happening. The close attention we pay in meditation allows us to become aware of feelings or emotions at an early stage. Allow your attention to go to this object and recognize that it is there. Give it a name if you can—for example "sleepiness," or "restlessness."

2 Acceptance

Once you have recognized this feeling, allow it to be there instead of trying to push it away or deny it (denial can make the feeling grow stronger). Try to welcome it and be open to it.

meditation is always to bring our beginner's mind to the experience. RAIN is an acronym for Recognition, Acceptance, Investigation, Nonidentification, the four steps in a systematic process for dealing with challenging states that arise in meditation or in daily life.

3 Investigation

Explore this feeling as if it is any other object of meditation—with kindly curiosity. What does it feel like? Where is it experienced in the body? What thoughts or stories are connected with it? Does it move or change? Does it seem to have a color or a shape?

4 Nonidentification

Be aware that this is a passing state—like all others—and does not define you. Acknowledge that there is a space between you, the witness to the emotion, and the challenging emotion itself. This distancing can also help the emotion to pass through you more quickly. It can help to say "restlessness is present" or "I notice restlessness," which has a different quality to "I am restless."

Where to Meditate

It is often said that you can meditate anywhere, and that's true. You can meditate on your morning commute, in a park during your lunch break, or waiting in line in the supermarket. But if you want to give your full attention to your practice, it makes sense to minimize the number of distractions around you. It is also helpful to practice in the same place each day.

When you practice regularly in the same space, that place can inspire and deepen your meditation. Passing your meditation spot can serve as a reminder to practice, just as work tasks spring to mind when you see your desk. And in time, simply entering this space may provide a sense of "arriving" or stillness. Having a familiar meditation spot can also reduce the tendency to be distracted; you probably won't become intrigued by, say, a mark on the wall if you see it every day.

A peaceful place

The place where you meditate should be peaceful. We cannot entirely control our environment, and part of meditation is accepting whatever arises. All the same, it makes sense to choose a place that is away from the hubbub. Choose a time when you can be alone to meditate, or ask anyone you live with to give you a few minutes' peace. And leave your cell phone somewhere else—any incoming calls and messages are sure to disturb you, and you will also want to avoid the temptation to check your mail or social media.

Meditating Outdoors

Meditating outdoors can be a beautiful way to connect with the wonder of the natural world, and many meditations are traditionally done in the open air. Try to choose an out-of-the-way spot where you won't be disturbed. As with meditating indoors, it can be helpful to sit in the same place, perhaps under a favorite tree or on a particular bench.

Light and air

If possible, avoid an area that gets too
hot or too cold, because extremes of
temperature can interfere with your focus.
It is wonderful to have some natural light
(if you are meditating in daylight hours),
but the brightness of direct sun can be
distracting, so make sure there are blinds
or drapes. Ideally, you'll be able to open
a window, because fresh air helps with
alertness.

CREATING YOUR SPACE

Dedicating an area of your home to meditation can help to inspire your practice and facilitate better concentration. How you arrange your meditation space is a personal decision, but it is best to keep it as clear and as simple as possible. Here are some guidelines that apply to most spaces.

1 Keep it clean and tidy

You can treat organizing your meditation space as a meditation practice in itself—see page 98 for mindful chores.

2 Have what you need

Include the chair or cushion you sit on, and have a shawl or sweater to keep warm, a nonticking clock so you can set an alarm, and perhaps a lamp for soft lighting.

3 Create a beautiful smell

Use incense, scented candles, or aromatherapy oils in a burner. These can foster a meditative atmosphere.

4 Consider sound

Most meditations are done in silence, but sometimes you may want to listen to soft music or other calming sounds—perhaps gentle running water.

5 Consider including a "shrine"

That word has religious connotations, but in this context it simply means a low table or shelf where you keep symbolic reminders of your meditation or its underlying purpose, things that can serve as an inspiration to practice or as a focal point.

Your shrine might include:

- *a beautiful cloth to lay on the surface*

- *a candle or two*

- *a spiritual image or icon, such as a picture of a saint or a statue of the Buddha*

- *a vase of fresh flowers or some token of nature, such as shells or pinecones*

- *a bell or singing bowl (see page 77)*

- *a string of beads (see pages 116 and 132–33).*

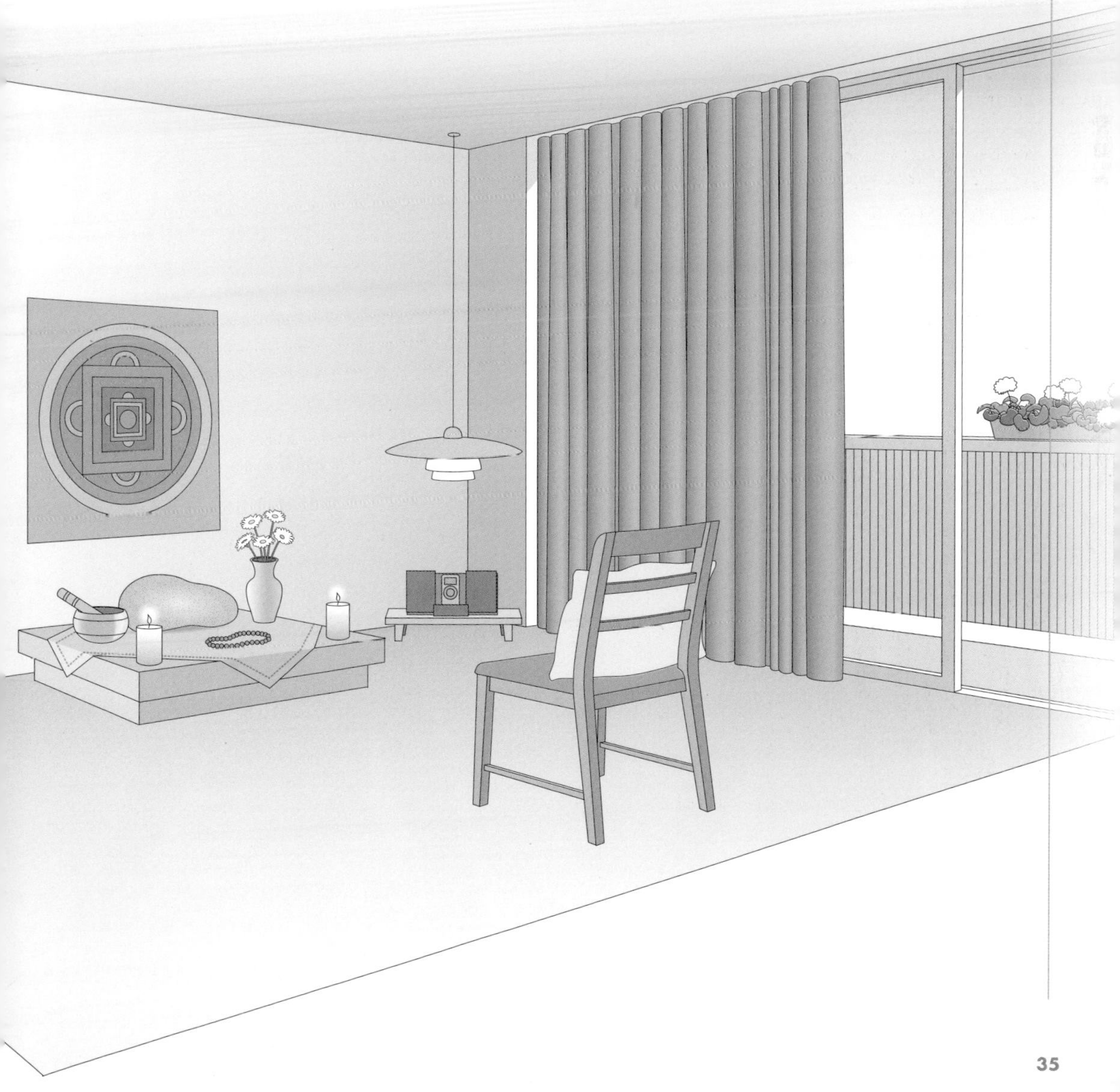

Postures for Meditation

All meditation requires your body to be in a strong and stable position. You need to feel relaxed enough to sustain the pose for a length of time, and you will also need to remain alert.

The Tripod of Support

The key thing to remember, no matter what you sit on, is that there should be three points of contact with the ground (the "tripod of support"): buttocks + knee + knee (cushion), buttocks + knee/shin + knee/shin (bench), or buttocks + sole of both feet (chair).

When your pose is comfortable, concentration comes more easily. All teachers emphasize the importance of keeping the spine upright. It is often likened to a tower of coins; the vertebrae should be neatly stacked on top of each other, while respecting the natural "S"-shape curvature of the spine.

Most meditations are practiced in a sitting posture, because this offers the best balance between comfort and alertness.

Loving the floor

In the West, we are used to sitting on couches and chairs, which encourages us to slump instead of using our muscles to hold us up. This can eventually lead to the shortening of the hamstrings and hip flexor muscles, weakening of the lower back, and straining of the shoulders and neck. Consequently, when we try to sit on the floor, it can feel uncomfortable or even painful. Many people lose interest in meditation because of this, but it is worth experimenting with different sitting positions and being prepared to adapt your posture to the needs of your body.

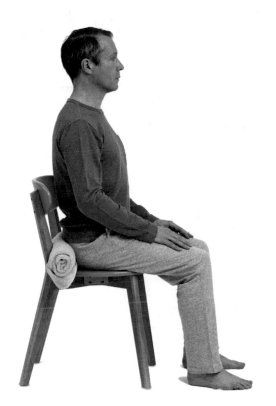

Experimenting with sitting

The classic meditation posture is the full lotus, but most of us cannot sustain this position without hurting ourselves. The Burmese position (see left), in which one bent leg is placed in front of the other, is easier to accomplish. Or you may find it best to sit in a simple cross-legged pose.

Using a cushion

Sitting on a hard floor requires a great deal of flexibility, so you should use a firm cushion or a folded towel to elevate your buttocks and place one under each knee if they don't reach the floor naturally. This provides a tripod of support that naturally grounds your body and facilitates an upright spine. If you have back problems or other issues that prevent you from sitting comfortably on the floor, you can use a meditation bench or simply sit on an upright chair. In the end, meditation is an exercise of the mind, not of the body, and the position you choose should be one that you can sustain for some time.

HOW TO SIT
Burmese pose, which is practiced throughout Southeast Asia, is one of the easiest sitting positions—but try the variations over the pages, too, to see what works best for you. Sit on a round meditation cushion (a zafu), an ordinary cushion, or a pillow folded in half. If the floor is hard, sit on a folded blanket or a flat square meditation cushion (a zabuton).

1 *Either sit on the front of the cushion (this helps keep your back upright) or in the middle of the cushion and roll your hips slightly forward.*

2 *Bend one leg, rotating at the hip to avoid placing pressure on your knees, and bring the side of the foot to rest in front of you.*

3 *Bend the other leg in the same way, resting the side of that foot in front of the first leg. When you meditate regularly, you should alternate which leg you place in front.*

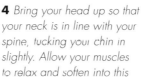

4 *Bring your head up so that your neck is in line with your spine, tucking your chin in slightly. Allow your muscles to relax and soften into this upright stance.*

5 *Rest your hands on your knees, or cup them in your lap. If you have shoulder pain, place a cushion in your lap to bring your hands higher.*

6 *Close your eyes, or look at a spot on the floor about three feet (a meter) in front of you, keeping your gaze soft.*

7 *Have your mouth closed or slightly open, to help you avoid clenching your teeth. Breathe through your nose. Resting your tongue just behind your front teeth on the hard palate helps to keep your jaw relaxed.*

Placing the Hands

Rest your hands on your lap or knees, choosing a position that facilitates the comfort of your hands, arms, and shoulders.

In this pose, the right hand rests on the left, thumbs touching. The thumbs will drift apart if you lose focus, or they will press too hard together if you apply too much effort, providing useful feedback.

Here, the thumb and index finger touch, forming a circle that symbolizes perfection and wholeness.

OTHER WAYS TO SIT
All these positions require you to keep your back upright, which is conducive to maintaining concentration. If you need support because of back problems, you can sit against a wall or the chair back or lie down.

Cross-legged pose
Sit on a firm cushion with your legs crossed in front of you. Each foot should rest under the knee of the opposite leg.

Half lotus
Follow the instructions for the Burmese position (see page 38), but have one foot under the thigh of the opposite leg and the second foot resting on the thigh of the first leg. Alternate which foot is on top each time you meditate.

Lotus pose
This is the pose used by the Buddha. The left foot rests on the right thigh and the right foot on the left thigh. If you are flexible enough to get into the pose comfortably, it provides great stability. Be sure to rotate your hip as you bend the leg, to avoid placing strain on the knee.

Kneeling pose

Sit on your heels with your knees together, and rest your hands on your lap. As with any sitting position, take a moment to lengthen your spine and then relax into the upright posture.

Kneeling with a seiza

Alternatively, use a seiza (meditation) bench, which takes the weight off your feet. Place the bench over your calves and then sit on it, so your lower legs are tucked underneath. If you don't have a seiza bench, turn a zafu or other firm cushion onto its edge, and then sit on it.

Sitting on a chair

Choose an upright chair with a flat seat, such as a dining chair (one that is the correct height for you). Have your feet flat on the floor, and sit toward the front of the chair so you are not tempted to lean back. Do not use the back of the chair for support at all; it can help to place a rolled-up towel between your body and the back of the chair (see page 36) so that the base of your back is supported but your body is prevented from drifting backward to the back of the chair.

STANDING & LYING DOWN POSTURES

You can meditate while standing or lying down as well as sitting. Meditating in a standing position is naturally energizing and can be a good way to resist boredom or sleepiness during meditation. Most people need to build up their stamina for standing, so begin by practicing for just a few minutes. Lying down sounds like the easiest way to meditate but is actually the most difficult, because the temptation to fall asleep can be overwhelming. However, it is a good option for anyone with severe back pain and can also be a good way to practice before sleep.

Lying down

1 *Lie on your back with your head on a thin pillow or a folded towel. Place a folded blanket underneath you if you are on a hard floor, or use a yoga mat.*

2 *Bend your legs and place your feet flat on the floor, roughly where your knees would be if your legs were extended—this helps to protect your lower back from strain. Have your arms by your sides, palms facing up or down as is comfortable for you.*

Standing posture

1 *Stand with your feet hips' width apart, toes pointing forward or slightly inward.*

2 *Keep the soles of your feet flat on the floor so that your weight is evenly distributed between the heels and balls, and the insides and outsides. Lift your toes and spread them as wide as you can before placing them back on the floor to create the most stable base possible.*

3 *Extend your spine completely. Visualize a string attached to the center of the top of your head and imagine pulling it up, and also down from the base of your spine, so that you lift the upper spine and drop the tailbone, creating a "tug" in both directions. Then allow yourself to relax into the position. Let your chin drop slightly so you feel a little lengthening in the neck—not too much or you will collapse the spine here.*

4 *Make sure your knees are slightly bent instead of locked straight. Bring the tailbone in slightly.*

5 *Keep your arms by your sides, hands hanging down. Or gently clasp them and rest them in front of your belly.*

When to Meditate

You can practice meditation whenever suits your schedule. Sitting before breakfast, when your mind is clear and you are well rested, is often recommended. It has the advantage of getting the day off to a peaceful start, but may you may need to get up earlier than the rest of the household.

Many people prefer to practice in the downtime of the evening, and meditating last thing at night can help you to wind down and promote good sleep. However, it is more probable that you will experience drowsiness. Try keeping your eyes open, or meditating standing up if you find yourself dozing off.

In the end, there is no set time to meditate. Whether lunchtime, mid-afternoon, or straight after work, they all work for someone. If possible, stick to the same time each day.

How long?

When you start out—and sometimes even when you have been meditating for years—two minutes can feel like an incredibly long time. It's best to start small and build up gradually, committing to a couple of minutes a day can be a more achievable aim than a 30-minute practice. You may find it helpful to do a short practice in the morning and one in the evening, or you may prefer to do a single longer practice. It is up to you to work out what is best. Decide how long you want to sit for before you start, and set a timer so that you don't need to keep checking the time.

Eating and drinking

It is important to avoid alcohol before meditating, because of its obvious effect on concentration. Many meditation teachers would also advise against taking other stimulants, such as coffee. A heavy meal can make you feel sluggish, so it is best not to practice straight after eating. Meditating on an empty stomach is often recommended, but if you are ravenous, then hunger itself becomes a distraction. So have a glass of milk or a small snack if you need it.

What to wear

Wear loose or nonrestrictive clothing, especially around the waist and knees; tight pants or skirts make it hard to sit on the floor. Most meditators like to have a shawl or sweater around their shoulders, because your body temperature drops when you sit still for a time. A shawl can also double up as a rest for your hands.

PREPARING THE BODY

Doing some gentle stretching or yoga is a good way to prepare your body for a lengthy period of sitting. Here are some simple stretches to try. You don't need to have done any yoga to do these, but you should not attempt them if you have an injury or restricted movement (or if you are pregnant) unless you know it is safe to do so. If you are sitting in a chair or find it hard to be on all fours for any reason, start from shoulder rolls. Work very gently, and do a few calm breaths before you start. Do not go to the edge of your capability; these movements should be gentle and easily achievable, not a full stretch.

All fours

1 *Go onto your hands and knees with your hands directly under your shoulders and your knees directly under your hips. Slowly drop your head, and as you do so, let your back arch up toward the ceiling and your tailbone drop. Take a conscious breath in this position.*

2 *Bring your head slowly up. Let the movement follow through your back so that it rounds down toward the floor and your tailbone rises. Move between the two poses slowly and smoothly two or three times, breathing deeply.*

Simple side stretch

1 *Now widen your knees and bring your buttocks back so you can sit on your heels. Bring your head to the floor, or rest your head on a cushion if that feels easier.*

2 *Slowly walk your hands to the left, letting your body turn to the side and feeling a stretch along the right. Spend a few moments breathing deeply in this position.*

3 *Then walk your hands back and to the right to stretch the other side.*

Shoulder rolls

1 *Slowly come up from the floor by walking your hands back toward your body. Assume your meditation position.*

2 *Bring your shoulders slowly up toward your ears, then roll them back.*

3 *With your head in a centered position, roll your shoulders in a circular motion while bringing your shoulder blades together to the original position.*

4 *Continue the circular movement, bringing your shoulders forward and up again. Work very slowly,*

coordinating the movement with your breath so you are inhaling on the upward motion and exhaling on the downward motion. Do this another two times, and then three times in the opposite direction.

Arm stretch

Bring your right arm up above your head, palm facing inward. Then slowly stretch over to the left as far as feels comfortable and stable. You can breathe in as you bring the arm up, and breathe out as you stretch, or just breathe normally as you do the exercise. Slowly come up to the center and then do the other side. Repeat another two times.

Hip Openers

If you are used to yoga, pigeon pose and butterfly pose are hip-opening postures that are helpful if you will be sitting for long periods.

Floor twist

Slowly turn to the left, putting your left hand on the floor behind you and resting your right hand on your left knee. Then come back to the

center, and go the other way. You don't need to go very far— remember that you are simply preparing the body for meditation instead of doing a full twist.

Chair side twist

Place your left palm against the outside of your right thigh and gently turn to look over your right shoulder (or in that direction if you find it difficult). Slowly come back to the center, release your hand, and repeat on the other side.

Back and forward bend

1 Tip your head gently back to look up at the ceiling, directly above and slightly behind you. This creates a slight backbend; move slowly and carefully to avoid compressing your neck.

2 Lower your head toward your chest, roll down your shoulders and fold forward as far as you are comfortable. Let your back round naturally as you come forward instead of trying to keep it straight. This is an easy one to do if you are sitting in a chair, too.

49

DEVELOPING AWARENESS

Meditation and awareness go hand in hand; you could say that meditation is the conscious cultivation of awareness. This chapter introduces you to exercises that have been practiced for thousands of years and all over the world. We begin with awareness of the breath, then move on to other ways that we can apprehend our moment-by moment-experience—using sound, body sensation, thoughts, and emotions as an object of attention. These techniques culminate in the more advanced method of choiceless—or open—awareness, in which you allow your attention to be drawn to whichever aspect of your experience is most apparent. The chapter gives advice on dealing with discomfort and includes aids that you can use in your meditation, including breath counting and noting (or labeling).

Awareness of the Breath

Know your breath
The Buddha's primary instructions for meditation were:
"Know I am breathing in, know I am breathing out. When I am taking a short breath, know I am taking a short breath; when I am taking a long breath, know I am taking a long breath."

Breathing occurs constantly and unconsciously; it is always with us. But, unusually among the body processes, it is also something that we can bring under our conscious control. By practicing awareness of the breath without trying to control it, we can learn how to be present in each moment as it unfolds.

We all know that breath changes in response to the actions of the body; when we are working hard, our breathing comes harder, and when we rest it slows. Breath also changes with the emotions;

when we are fearful, the breath is shallow, and when we feel frustrated, we might expel the breath forcefully. And it changes with our state of mind; when we focus intently on a task we may hold our breath, and when we are highly agitated, we might find it hard to breathe at all.

So at any given moment, the breath can provide insight into body, mind, and emotion. As we become more adept at focusing on the breath, we can gain awareness of inward experiences as they arise.

Gateway to understanding

Awareness of the breath features in many spiritual traditions, and it is one of the key Buddhist teachings. The Buddha saw practicing meditations on the breath as a gateway to enlightenment, and this is echoed in other spiritual traditions and cultures. In many languages, the words for "breath" and "spirit" are related or the same.

Letting go of the breath

When we meditate, there is a temptation to take charge of the breath, perhaps to make it easier to discern, or because we feel it is better to breathe deeply. But in awareness meditation, the point is simply to watch what is occurring without interference, like you might watch water flowing down a stream or a flame flickering. Let each breath unfold, following its own rhythm.

This can be harder than it sounds, almost impossible at first. Understanding how difficult it is to let go is itself a valuable insight. And with continued practice, it becomes easier.

BELLY-WATCHING MEDITATION

Belly watching is taught in Taoist meditation, as well as in Zen and other Buddhist traditions. When you focus on the involvement of your belly in breathing, your breath will naturally begin to deepen and slow down, so this meditation can also feel calming. The belly is often the easiest place to discern the breath, so this is a good exercise for beginners.

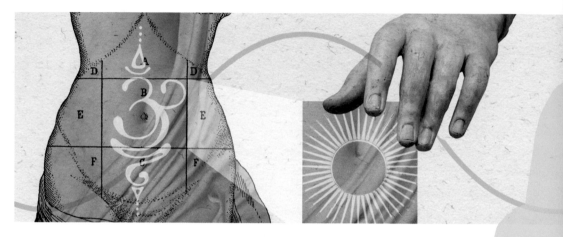

1 Get into a comfortable sitting position. You can practice this meditation lying down if you have back or other pain, but belly breathing can incline you toward sleepiness, so it is better to sit if you can.

2 Close your eyes and take a couple of deep, slow breaths before you start. Place your hands on your lap (or by your sides if you are lying down.) Photo: have the palms facing up

3 Breathe through your nose, letting the breath find its pathway into your body and out again. As you breathe in, bring your awareness to your belly rising. Then, as you breathe out, be aware of your belly falling. Simply focus all your attention on this movement: the rising motion in your belly as you breathe in, the falling motion as you breathe out. You may want to say "rising" silently to yourself on the upward movement, and "falling" on the downward to help you concentrate.

4 Try narrowing your focus to a spot in your belly that is 1½ inches below and behind the navel (this is known as the "lower dantian" in Taoist meditation). Placing a hand on your belly can help your attention remain on the movement.

5 You may become aware that your focus has drifted. Without judging yourself for your stray thoughts, come back to the sensations in the belly. Do this as many times as you need to—it may be once, several times, or a hundred times.

6 At the end of the meditation, gently release your focus. Slowly open your eyes and rest for a few moments before getting up.

WATCHING THE BREATH

In this meditation, the aim is to bring your focus to the tip of the nostrils or the upper lip. The exact spot varies from person to person; it is wherever you feel the breath most distinctly. This is a more subtle sensation than the movement of the belly, so it encourages deep concentration.

1 *Get into an upright and comfortable position on the floor or the chair and close your eyes. Enjoy a couple of long, deep breaths to help settle yourself into your seat.*

2 *Bring your attention to your nostrils. As you breathe in through your nose, be mindful of a slight sensation of coldness as the air passes the nostrils. Know that you are breathing in.*

3 *As you breathe out, you may also be able to discern the subtle sensation of the breath leaving the nostrils. This can be difficult to catch, but be aware that you are breathing out.*

As we practice focusing on the breath, we may notice that each breath is slightly different. The more we practice, the more we start to realize that even in a process as simple and natural as breathing there is a wealth of possibilities to experience.

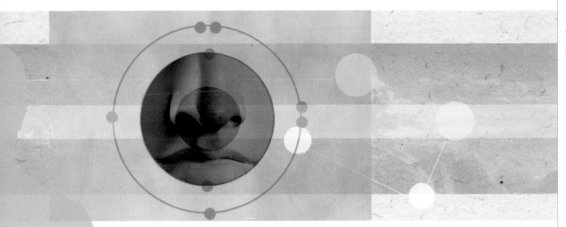

4 In time, you may notice a tiny pause between the in breath and the out breath, and again between the out breath and the in breath. Just be aware of this fleeting stillness and let the new in breath or out breath begin in its own time.

5 If you find yourself tensing, want the breath to be different, or long for the experience to be over, simply direct your attention back to the tip of your nostrils and continue to know that you are breathing in and breathing out.

Improving Focus

The idea of following the breath sounds easy, but a minute's practice reveals that it is very difficult. Why? Because most of us are not used to focusing in such a singular way. Most people require sustained practice to follow the breath for any length of time. In the meantime, we begin over and again. As soon as you notice that your attention has wandered, gently guide it back to the breath.

Stepping back

Conversely, concentrating too hard on the simple act of breathing—something that our body does spontaneously, naturally,

all our lives—can have the effect of making it feel awkward and forced. In meditation, the idea is to step back a little to observe the breath calmly instead of intensively, to develop a sense of ourselves as witness to whatever sensations and processes are occurring in the body.

Useful aids

There are various ways that you can help your focus. Noting the breath—for example, "in" and "out" as you inhale and exhale, or "rising" and "falling" if you are doing the belly-watching meditation—is one method. Another is counting. In this

method, you silently count the breaths from one to ten, and then start again instead of continuing on to larger numbers.

Breath counting helps to give your practice a sense of structure and purpose—you have a goal of ten to reach and then must change tack. The number doesn't have to be ten, of course—you could count to five or eight or twenty. But ten is a natural quantity, the number of fingers on the hands, so we use it here.

Variations of breath counting

You can count both the in breath and the out breath (one, two), or you can count only the in breath or only the out breath. If you are feeling sluggish, counting the in breath can help to increase your alertness. If you are feeling agitated or find yourself hurrying the breath in order to count, focusing on the out breath can create a greater sense of relaxation. Try to inculcate a sense of letting go as you breathe out.

COUNTING THE BREATH

Breath counting is taught in some Zen and other Buddhist traditions. It is very easy to do, and it is the kind of simple do-anywhere practice that you can use as a stress management technique as well as a meditation. Breathe through your nose and let the breath find its natural rhythm, whether that is long or short, deep or shallow.

1 *Take a few moments to settle into a comfortable sitting position.*

2 *Breathe in, and at the end of the inhalation, make the mental note "one."*

3 *Breathe out, and at the end of the exhalation, count "two." Continue until you reach ten.*

Mind Aid

If you find it difficult to practice breath counting, use your fingers as a counting aid. For the first count of one, softly hold the thumb of your left hand with the thumb and fingers of your right hand. Then move on to the index finger for two and so on; switch hands when you get to six. When you feel more confident, release the hands and return to counting the breaths.

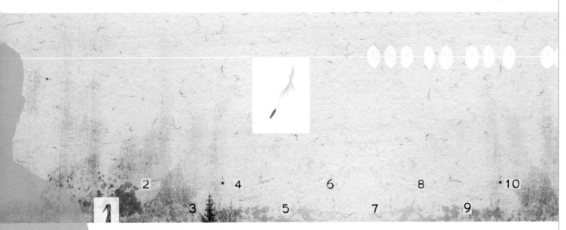

2   • 4   6   8   •10
1   3   5   7   9

4 If you notice that you are trying to control the breath, it can help to make your counting gentle. If you are losing focus or finding the exercise boring, add a little more clarity and strength to the numbering. You may want to whisper the number out loud, too.

5 If at any point you forget the number you are on, or become distracted, start at one again. Sometimes you may find it difficult to get past "two," but keep starting again at one as often as you need to, trying to release any sense of judgment or frustration.

6 When you can reach ten easily, switch to counting each breath cycle. Breathe in and out, count one, breathe in and out, count two, and so on up to ten before starting again. Eventually you should be able to drop the breath counting, and focus on simple awareness of the breath.

Awareness of the Body

Sensations arise in the body all the time—pleasant ones, unpleasant ones, neutral ones. In day-to-day life, we are too busy or distracted to notice these unless they become intense. That's why we may continue keying at a computer or digging in the garden despite warning signals that we are causing damage. Or why we may routinely clench the jaw, or sit in a posture that gives us backache.

Body, mind, emotions

Our body posture and mental state and emotions are linked. When we are feeling vulnerable, we may sit in a slumped position, making the body as small as possible; whereas when we feel confident, our stance may be broad and tall. Psychological experiments show that the reverse is also true. Simply standing in an upright posture with shoulders back and feet firmly planted on the floor (the "power pose") can make us feel more in control. Conversely, adopting a defensive posture—hunched shoulders, head down—can evoke feelings of anxiety or depression.

A key technique

Awareness of the body is a key meditation used in mindfulness training and in the general Buddhist tradition. Together with awareness of the breath, sounds, emotions, and thoughts, it helps us to build the receptive awareness that lets us connect with our moment-by-moment experience.

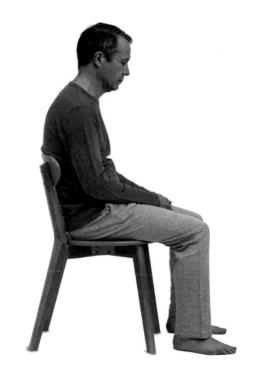

Open awareness

In meditation, we strip away stimuli, in order to concentrate more completely. You can practice an open and fluid awareness of the body by assuming your meditation posture and waiting for sensations to arise. When one does, give it your attention and investigate it. When another sensation calls your attention, bring your focus here, investigating it with an attitude of kindly curiosity as it shifts under your mental gaze.

A whole-body awareness can be difficult to sustain if your mind is unsettled or if you are a beginner in meditation. In these cases, a more systematic body-awareness meditation, such as body sweeping (see the following pages), may suit you better. This involves attending to one area of the body after another, in turn, and is a good way to foster greater body awareness generally.

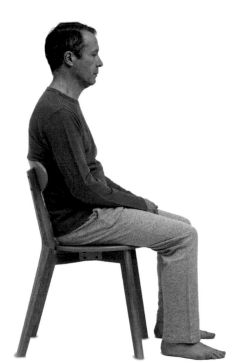

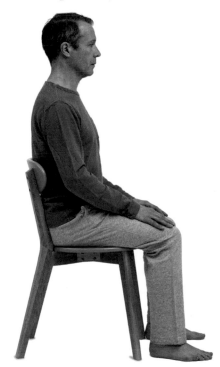

BODY SWEEPING

This is a classic meditation technique—used in the Buddhist tradition—in which you explore the sensations of the body by sweeping your attention from toe to head (or vice versa). This helps to release tension and builds awareness of the body. In mindfulness practice, it's sometimes known as the body scan.

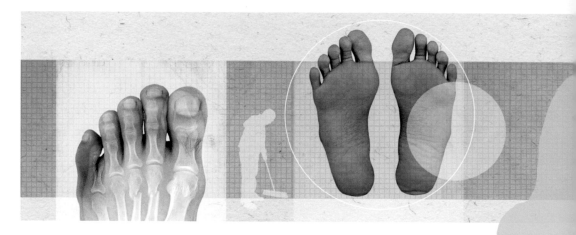

1 *Sit in your preferred meditation position, and softly close your eyes. Take some deep breaths and relax into the present moment, letting go of anything that has happened before this point. You may want to practice awareness of the breath for a few moments.*

2 *Now bring your full attention to your toes. Become aware of any sensation here—a tingling, heaviness, lightness, coolness, touch. If you do not feel anything, just notice the absence of feeling. Whatever sensation is there, let it be without judging it or trying to change it, and then let your attention move on.*

3 *Slowly bring your focus to the soles of your feet, simply noticing any sensation in them. After the soles, move to the sides and the tops of your feet. You can do both feet at the same time, or one, and then the other—whichever feels easier.*

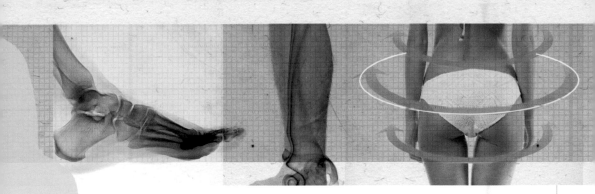

4 Rest your attention on your ankles, which carry the weight of your body. What sensations do you feel here? Simply become aware of them, then shift your attention to the next spot.

5 Continue up your legs: calves and shins, knees, and thighs. Whatever sensation there is—hardness, softness, openness, tightness—notice it and then move on to the next part of your body. If you are finding it hard to concentrate, try silently labeling the part of the body you are investigating—for example "knees" or "thighs."

6 Now move to your groin, genital area, buttocks, hips, being aware of each region as your attention rests on it, noticing what sensations are there and then, once you have become aware of one or more, moving on to the next area.

Continued overleaf

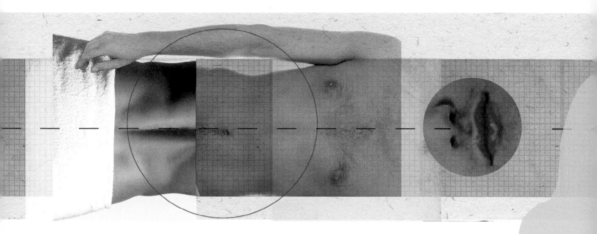

7 Shift your attention to the abdomen, the lower back, then the chest, spending as long as is necessary on each area until you become aware of a sensation or absence of sensation. You don't have to analyze or name the sensation—all you are doing is noticing it.

8 Become aware of the shoulders, so often a source of tension. What do you feel here? Aching, obstruction, contraction, or expansion? Sweep your attention down the arms—the upper arms, the elbows, the lower arms, and wrists—before noticing the sensations in the hands.

9 Now focus your full attention on the neck and throat, then move up to the face: the jaw, the mouth, the upper lip and nostrils, the cheeks, ears, eyes, forehead. You may notice sensations on the surface of the skin, or inside your body. There is no need to look for anything in particular; simply notice what is there.

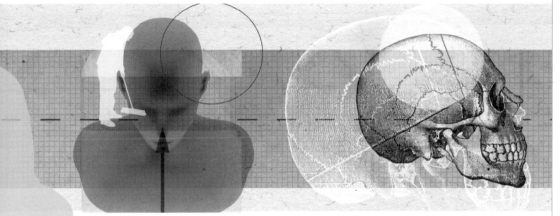

10 *Finally, sweep your attention over the back of the head and the top of the head, picking up any sensation there, whatever it is.*

11 *Rest for a few moments, being aware of the body as a whole, before ending the meditation. Try to bring this awareness of the body with you as you get up slowly.*

Adapting the Meditation

This is a versatile technique that you can practice almost anywhere. If you are short of time, you can focus on wider areas of your body: the whole feet, the ankles and lower legs, the thighs and buttocks, the torso, the shoulders and arms, the neck and head. Or you can do a quick sweep at the start of any meditation to make contact with the body and settle into the present moment.

If you prefer, start at the top of your body and sweep downward, or perhaps start at the top and sweep down, and then sweep back up.

Dealing with Discomfort

As soon as we begin to meditate, we start to become much more aware of small sensations in the body, such as itching, aching, pressure. It is human nature to try to push away any difficulty or negative sensation, to try to get rid of it. So as soon as we feel an itch, we scratch; the smallest ache, we wriggle or shift our position to make it more comfortable. Or perhaps we sit, noticing it and hating it. And the more we hate it, the more tension and dislike we bring to it, the more intense the sensation may become.

Investigating sensations

It's often advised to sit with discomfort—and this can be a useful practice. When a sensation pulls at your attention, you can try giving it your focus with a sense of generosity instead of ignoring it or wishing it away. When you do this, notice the very human impulse to do something in order to change the sensation—to scratch an itch or shift position. Instead of acting on this urge, try exploring both the feeling and the impulse to act, noticing how even an intense sensation can change under the spotlight of your inner gaze before fading away.

Moving with kindness

Sometimes pain can dissolve when we investigate it in this way. Having said that, we do not aim to sit with an attitude of endurance; we want to treat our bodies with kindness. If you are gritting your teeth and longing for your meditation period to be over because of discomfort, then you are not meditating—you are simply suffering in silence. And it is possible to hurt yourself in meditation if you continue to maintain a posture that is putting strain on your body. In these instances, move to ease your pain. But move consciously and deliberately, instead of fidgeting. Using the noting technique on pages 70–71 can help you to adjust your posture without disturbing your equilibrium.

Judging discomfort

It's not always easy to tell whether you are experiencing true discomfort or a temporary sensation that you can work with. Experimenting with this is part of our meditation practice in which we are learning to see what sensations can be investigated and which ones cause an unhelpful attitude of endurance.

NOTING THE MOVEMENTS
Noting or labeling is taught in Burmese tradition. It gives the thinking mind something to do and, like counting, is used to support our focus and prevent spacing out. If you are uncomfortable in meditation, and you need to adjust your position or scratch, noting can help you to maintain a concentrated attitude.

1 *Sit in your preferred position and focus on the breath wherever you feel it most strongly—in the belly, or at the nostrils, or perhaps in the chest.*

2 *At some point, a physical sensation will become strong enough to get your attention—say, an itch or a pain. Give it your focus. If it disappears, return to the breath. If it intensifies and then shifts and disappears, also return to the breath. But if the sensation is intense and you want to scratch (or move):*

- *First label the feeling as "pain" or "itching" or just "feeling."*

- *Before you move, notice that there is an impulse to move— label it as "urge to move."*

- *Now move, labeling it as "moving." When you become more adept at doing this, you can label each part of the movement: "raising" the arm, "moving," "lowering" the arm.*

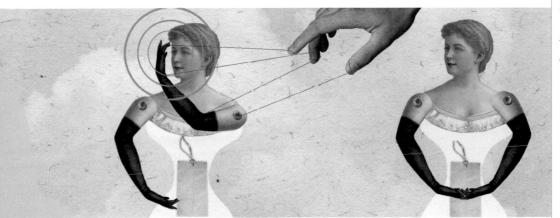

- Then scratch, making the note "scratching" or simply "moving."

- Notice the intention to move the hand back: "urge to move."

- Move the hand back, labeling it as "moving" or labeling all the constituent parts.

- As you bring the hand back to your lap, label it as "placing."

3 Resume focusing on the breath.

Noting the Constituent Parts

You can practice noting in everyday life—Burmese monks do it from their waking breath. If you are about to go through a door, you could note: "intending to move," "raising" the hand, "moving" the hand forward, "touching" the doorknob, "grasping" the doorknob, "turning" the doorknob, "pushing" the doorknob. It's interesting to take a small movement and see how you can label the constituent parts—try doing it for making a cup of coffee.

A World of Sound

Accepting the moment
*It's common to feel irritated when
your silent meditation is disturbed.
But experiencing sound is part of
the moment, too.*

When we sit down to meditate, we choose to do it in a quiet place, so that we are not distracted. But we soon realize that we are always surrounded by sound. If you stop to listen right now, you will find that the world is a pretty noisy place, alive with traffic noise, voices, the low hum of a computer or air conditioner, the bubbling of a radiator—and at the very least, the sound of your own breath.

A gateway to the present

We can use the fact that sound is always there by making it into something that can help us cultivate an attitude of awareness and receptivity. Hearing (like all the senses) is a gateway between the external and the internal, because sounds that originate outside of ourselves are experienced moment by moment as vibrations inside the ear. So consciously bringing our attention to sound helps us to step into the here and now.

The art of hearing

When we practice awareness of sound, we try to focus on the experience of receiving sounds instead of trying to listen for anything in particular. We notice the quality, tone, volume, and sensation of the sound, instead of analyzing it.

We soon discover that this is difficult. And as we notice this difficulty, we can gain insights into the way the mind works. We become aware of its tendency to analyze everything it comes into contact with. A sound occurs and, quick as a flash, the mind names it: barking dog, church bell, footsteps. With these labels can come judgment—this sound is pleasant, that sound is unpleasant—or emotions, such as irritation, pleasure, anxiety. It may trigger stories—for example, a dog bark may remind you of a childhood pet. Very quickly, you may become lost in a flood of memories.

When we practice awareness of sound, we maintain a receptive openness, and we keep bringing our attention back to the pure experience of sound with the same attitude of nonjudgmental, curious interest that we bring to other forms of awareness practice.

AWARENESS OF SOUND

You can use sounds as an anchor for your attention just as you can use the breath, thoughts, emotions, or body sensations. The key principle is to focus your attention on the experience of receiving sound—on hearing—instead of on labeling or categorizing the sound itself.

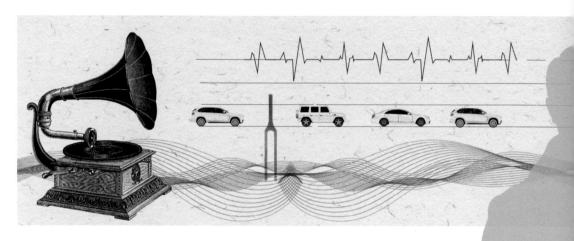

1 *Relax into your meditation posture, and bring your attention to your breathing wherever it is clearest, feeling the coolness of your breath at the nostrils, or the rising and falling sensation at the belly or chest. Focus on one breath at a time.*

2 *When your mind feels relatively settled, gently let your attention broaden to encompass sounds that are in and around you—the sounds of the body, the sounds of the room, the sounds from outside.*

3 *Be aware of the impulse to mentally reach out toward a sound. For example, if you hear the faint hum of traffic in the distance, watch your mind's focus travel to the source of the noise. Let go of this tendency to reach and grasp a sensory impression. Instead, focus on the internal experience of receiving the sound.*

4 Notice the tendency to name the sound. Our minds like to put a label on things—"traffic"— instead of simply hearing the low hum or roar. Perhaps we notice a judgment that the sound is appealing or unappealing, or a feeling of irritation or pleasure. Try to let go of such judgments, and focus on the pure experience.

5 Hear, too, the spaces in between the sounds. Subtler sounds may enter these spaces— perhaps the gentle thud of your own heartbeat.

6 If you find yourself distracted, gently recognize this, too—and return your focus to the experience of hearing.

NADA YOGA MUSIC MEDITATION This meditation is a

different way to practice awareness of sound. It is drawn from a Hindu practice of deep listening called nada yoga, in which you aim to tune in to your own inner sound. External (ahata) nada yoga is a preliminary exercise that anyone can do. All you need is a track of instrumental music and a music device.

1 *Turn off any devices other than the music player and get into your preferred meditation posture. Take a few deep breaths and let your body relax on the out breath.*

2 *Turn on the music, and close your eyes. Let yourself open up to the sounds of the music.*

3 *Notice if your body has reactions to the sounds. Perhaps there is a tensing or relaxing of muscle, a fluttering or prickling in the chest area or belly.*

Singing Bowl

For a short version of this meditation, strike a "singing bowl" or pluck a note on a string instrument. Focus on the sound you hear until it gradually fades away.

Mind the Volume

Keep the volume high enough so that you can hear it without straining, but do not let it blast out. It is better to experience the music as ambient sound than it is to use headphones that direct it to the ears. As you become more familiar with this exercise, you can reduce the volume to cultivate a greater capacity of deep listening.

4 *If the music is familiar to you, you may find yourself anticipating the next few bars or an upcoming key change—some future event in the piece. If this happens, guide your attention back to the now, to the musical sounds that are happening in this instant.*

5 *Perhaps thoughts arise. Music can trigger a stream of associations and memories. Or you may find yourself thinking about the music itself. Again, when you notice this, gently direct your attention back to the present.*

The Monkey Mind

Eastern Buddhist teachers talk of the monkey mind, meaning how the attention leaps from one thought to another, just as monkeys leap from one branch to the next. In meditation, we learn to still our monkey mind by giving it something to focus on. And we can also use thoughts as an object of focus, bringing the same attitude of kindly curiosity to them that we do to any of our other moment-by-moment experiences.

When we observe our thoughts in this way, we can start to find the space between them and ourselves. We start to realize that instead of being something we can control, most of our thoughts are simply products of the mind that arise, are present, and then pass away without our consciously doing anything at all.

Releasing our thoughts

In time, this can help us to realize that we do not have to be in thrall to our thoughts and stories, or let them drive our actions, no matter how persistent they are (although, of course, we may consciously choose for them to do so). Instead of berating ourselves for the things that go on in our minds, we can see our thoughts as just thoughts. In the end, meditation is not about controlling or changing your thoughts—it is about developing a different relationship with them.

Awareness of emotions

You can use the same technique to observe any emotions that arise: stopping and observing them, investigating where they are felt in the body, noting whether they have a shape or texture. When we notice and acknowledge our feelings, we are taking a step toward a kind of liberation. This is because getting to know ourselves can help set us free from the reactive nature of our behavior.

Nonthinking

As an experiment, try sitting down for two minutes and practicing nonthinking—preventing any thoughts from arising. You can use any method you want to help you to do this—try staring at a blank wall. At the end of two minutes, reflect on how you did. Almost certainly, you will have found that it is impossible to empty the mind of thoughts.

THOUGHTS AS CLOUDS
We often treat our thoughts as facts. However, when we practice mindful awareness we start to realize that they are, in fact, just figments. They come and go, and they are as transient and insubstantial as wispy clouds. Practicing awareness of thoughts can help us to gain a little distance, and it can help to release us from their grip on us.

1 *Sit in a comfortable pose, with your back straight. Take a couple of deep breaths to relax into your posture and come into the present moment, finding a sense of your body as it is right now.*

2 *Focus on the passing of the breath in and out of the body. You can focus on the nostrils or the belly, wherever you feel the sensation most strongly. Now turn your attention to your thoughts. You may find that there are no thoughts to attend to. However, "I can't do this," "I am not thinking anything," and "This is silly" are all thoughts.*

3 *As an experiment in thought watching, let your mind turn to something that is occurring in your life right now. It could be a pleasant, unpleasant, or neutral event, but it is better to choose something that does not provoke deep emotion in you.*

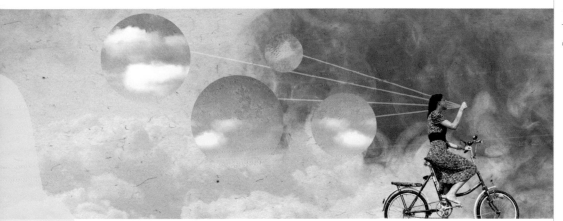

4 Notice that thoughts arise, are present, and then fade away. Be aware of how, when you bring your attention to one thought, it passes and another arises. They may be trivial, or they may be significant. It doesn't matter. All you need do is observe them.

5 You may want to imagine your thoughts as clouds—they may change shape as they scud across the sky. Or you might see them as leaves floating down a stream. The main point is, they will come and go.

6 Return your focus to the breath for a short period before ending the meditation.

AWARENESS OF EMOTIONS
Just as we cannot control our thoughts, neither can we prevent emotions from arising. All we can do is explore our relationship with them—whether we try to cling to them or push them away—and how we express them. Naming emotions, using the noting tool, can be an effective technique to help us step back from them and loosen their grip on us.

1 *Practice this meditation in conjunction with the "thoughts as clouds" meditation. Begin by focusing on the breath and then bring your attention to your thoughts. Watch them come and go like waterbirds on a river or clouds in the sky.*

2 *If the stirring of an emotion draws your attention (it may or may not be connected to a thought), bring your focus to it. Try to explore it, noticing where it is felt in the body, how it moves and changes, and how it strengthens or weakens as you investigate it. As far as you are able, try to bring a quality of gentle interest to your exploration.*

3 *Do not try to block or push away or change this feeling; instead, make room for whatever it is, pleasant or unpleasant, simply letting it be present and move through the body in its own way.*

4 *Notice any thoughts of judgment or criticism that come and let them go—you can label them "judging" or "thinking." Likewise, notice any urge to move or act. Can you make space for whatever is happening in your experience of this moment, without needing it to be different? This is the essence of awareness practice.*

See page 164 for dealing with intense emotions.

Use a Trigger

If you find it hard to notice emotions, try thinking about an event that brings up emotion in you—something sad, a pleasurable day, your favorite activity, or a dear friend. Visualize this event or person and then explore the feelings that arise in you.

THE HALF SMILE

When we meditate, we may notice that our inner voice is harsh and critical. It may be surprising to realize just how often your mental voice berates or insults you for the simplest of things—becoming distracted, thinking a thought, feeling a feeling. The half smile is a practical technique that can help to bring softness to your practice, letting you observe your thoughts and emotions with a sense of ease.

1 *Sit with your back straight and gently close your eyes. Spend a few moments getting in touch with the physical sensations of the body, particularly the feelings of pressure or contact where it rests on the floor or chair.*

2 *Take a deep breath in, and as you breathe out, let yourself relax into your meditation posture, knowing you are supported by the floor or chair.*

3 *With your mouth closed, curve your lips into a slight smile. Bring your attention to this area of the body, noticing any sense of relaxation here.*

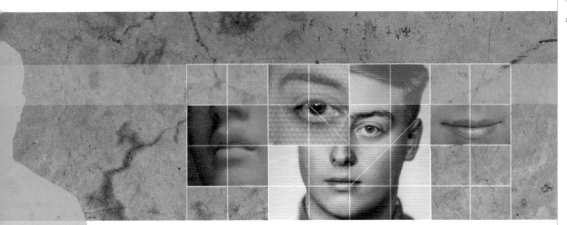

4 As you keep your attention on the mouth area, be aware of any sense that the smile is traveling upward and outward, across the cheeks and toward the eyes. You can track this with labels if you want: "My lips are smiling," "My cheeks are smiling," or "My eyes are smiling."

5 Breathe freely, then gently release your attention from your smile and bring it to your thoughts and feelings, or whatever other object of attention you are using. However, maintain the smile.

6 If you notice that the smile is becoming forced, or has disappeared, it can be a sign that you are tensing or getting carried away by your thoughts and feelings. Notice that, then come back to where you started. The half smile does not prevent thoughts and feelings from arising, but it can make it easier to sit back from and observe them.

Expanding Your Awareness

Open awareness is a practice in which we have no specific object for our awareness; instead we give our attention to whatever arises in the present moment—without applying any element of choice or control.

This practice derives from the teachings of the Buddha, and it is taught in several traditions, including mindfulness and Japanese Zen, where it is known as *shikantaza*, or "just sitting." It is often called "choiceless awareness," a term coined by the Indian teacher Jiddu Krishnamurti. You could also call it "the here-and-now meditation."

Objectless meditation

The reason we usually choose a focus for our meditation practice, such as the breath, is to provide an anchor for our busy mind. When we dispense with having a particular focus, the mind is free to attend to whatever arises. So we may notice first the breath, and then we may be drawn by a body sensation, a sound, a fluttering of emotion, or a thought.

As we observe our moment-to-moment experience in this way, without judging or trying to change, we can experience a sense of deep acceptance of what is.

We may also notice how one aspect of our experience can set off a train of others: a body sensation (say, an ache) triggers a thought ("Ah, that's painful"), which in turn triggers a feeling (perhaps irritation), then another thought ("I'm going to have to move"), then perhaps a physical act of tensing, which then increases the feeling of discomfort. In this way, we start to see how one aspect of our experience impacts on the next, and how our reactions can create discomfort for ourselves.

Working with distraction

It is far more difficult to sit with an expansive broad awareness than a narrower focus, and it is best to try it only when you have developed a degree of steadiness in other awareness practices (such as awareness of the breath). Even then, you may find that distraction can be more of an issue or you may have a sense of zoning out. If you find choiceless awareness challenging, try returning to one of the other awareness practices.

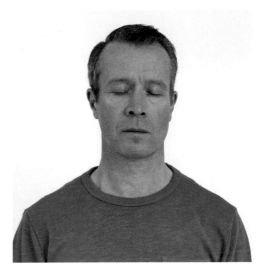

OPEN AWARENESS MEDITATION

In this meditation, our focus is awareness itself. We let our mind rest on whatever experience is calling: the breath, a thought, a feeling, a sound. It can be helpful to view this meditation as an open door. Instead of controlling what comes through the "door" of your focus, you welcome anything and everything that enters.

1 *Take a moment to relax into a comfortable sitting posture, either on the floor or on a chair. Take a couple of deep, slow breaths. Close your eyes.*

2 *Bring your focus to the body. You can do a full body sweep or simply direct your attention to the areas of the body that make contact with your support, noticing any heaviness or pressure. Then broaden your focus to include the whole body. Spend a minute on being aware only of the body.*

3 *When your mind feels steady, release this focus on the body. Let your awareness expand to encompass all aspects of your experience. Do not search for something to notice, but simply allow whatever arises to arise.*

4 *Let your attention dance between the breath, the sounds, the feelings, the thoughts. When something pulls at your attention, let the mind settle on it, and then let it go when the next object calls your attention or the first fades away. Sometimes this object will be ephemeral and will evaporate as soon as your focus goes there; at other times, something will hold your attention for longer.*

5 *If you find yourself distracted, be aware of this and then expand your awareness once again. You may find it helpful to ask yourself at intervals: "Where is my awareness?" or simply "Where is my mind?"*

6 *Before closing the meditation, return to awareness of the body for a few moments.*

OUTDOOR MEDITATION

It can often be easier to cultivate a sense of presence when in the fresh air. Buddhist monks—and the Buddha himself—often withdrew to forests or mountains to find the seclusion and simplicity they needed to go farther in their meditation. The Thai Forest Tradition grew out of this custom, and many monasteries today are sited in forests.

1 *Find a secluded spot in a natural setting—by a stream, under a tree, on top of a hill.*

2 *Settle into your meditation posture and close your eyes. Be aware of the parts of the body that are in contact with the ground; perhaps move your hand and touch the grass. Notice the coolness of the breeze or the warmth of the sun on your cheeks and skin. Try to notice only the qualities of the sensations you feel instead of analyzing them.*

3 *Gradually tune into the sounds of nature—perhaps a whisper of leaves as they move, the burbling of a stream, the buzz of an insect. Focus on the experience of receiving these sounds as you let yourself rest in the here and now.*

The Power of Awe

Research has shown that contemplating an impressive natural phenomenon induces a sense of awe, which can improve our levels of life satisfaction and make us feel like we have more time. It seems that being reminded of the vastness of our world gives us back our perspective.

4 *Gently open your eyes and, without moving your head, experience the sights that fall within your gaze. Notice the shapes, colors, textures—the quality of what you can see. The mind will come up with its labels: "grass," "tree," "oh, that's a pretty color." Simply acknowledge any thoughts that pull at your attention, then bring it back to the experience of observing.*

5 *Rest in this experience of being present, letting your awareness encompass the sounds, sights, and feelings of this natural setting as it changes from moment to moment.*

MEDITATION IN ACTION

This chapter shows you how to bring meditative awareness—or mindfulness—into all your daily activities. It begins with walking meditation, as taught by the Buddha. You may want to integrate it into your daily routine, or alternate walking and sitting meditations. Or you can simply introduce mindfulness into any short walk you do during the day. Also in this chapter are exercises that can transform your experience of ordinary activities, such as eating or even doing chores. Here, too, is a range of micromeditations that you can do throughout the day—from the moment you wake up to when you wind down for sleep. Some are intended for at home, some can be done at work or even in the gym.

Walking Meditation

Walking meditation is taught in many traditions, and it is a beautiful practice for beginners and advanced practitioners alike. Many people find it easier than sitting practice, especially if they are new to meditation; physical activity naturally draws our attention more easily than, say, the subtle sensations of the breath. Traditionally, monks and nuns alternate between the stillness of sitting practice and more active walking meditation—a format followed in many meditation retreats.

Formal practice

In walking meditation, we bring our focus to the act of stepping. To help us attend to the journey instead of the destination, we find a circumscribed pathway that is 15 to 30 feet (5–10 meters) long and we walk up and down it, staying aware of every step. There is no set pace, and no special movements are required. It is however, generally easier to attend to the sensations if you move slowly.

Like all forms of meditation, walking practice involves an element of skillfulness. At first, it can feel awkward, but as you practice, you will start to notice the many refined sensations involved in stepping. In time, you can incorporate your experience of walking meditation into daily life.

Different techniques

The simplest way to practice walking meditation is to focus on the contact between the soles of your feet and the ground. Practicing in bare feet lets you experience this more fully. Be aware of this contact, the feeling of pressure when one foot is in contact with the floor, and the corresponding pressure on the other foot when the first is lifted. If your attention wanders, gently bring it back to this feeling of pressure or contact.

Noting

When you feel comfortable with this
technique, try expanding your awareness
to different actions of the foot and leg:
lifting, moving, placing. You can use the
noting tool (see pages 70–71) to help
you focus. In time, you can start to note
more components of stepping: raising,
lifting, moving, dropping, placing,
pressing. But your focus should always
be on the experience of walking, not
the labeling. If the labeling becomes
a distraction, then return to a simple
awareness of contact.

WALKING PRACTICE

Choose a private spot up to 30 feet (10 meters) long for your walking path—a hallway or perhaps a lawn. Once you are comfortable, you may want to practice walking meditation in a park or other public place. Choose a quiet area so you won't be distracted by feeling watched or worrying what others are thinking. Walk for 10 minutes and build up to 30 or 60 minutes over time.

1 *Stand with your feet hips' width apart, arms by your side. Take a moment to experience standing. Notice the contact between your feet and the floor and let your shoulders, arms, legs, and body relax. Have your head in line with your spine, with your chin slightly dropped downward; your gaze should be at a point about 5 feet (1.5 meters) in front of you.*

2 *Before taking the first step, notice the intention to do so. Then, keeping your attention on the sole of your foot, lift your heel slowly from the ground, noticing how your weight shifts forward onto the ball of your foot.*

3 *Continue lifting your foot and then move it forward.*

Do a Count

If you feel distracted, try counting your steps (count from one to ten, and then start at one again). Alternatively, synchronize the steps with your breath, allowing for a full inhalation and exhalation for each step.

4 *Place your foot on the ground, noticing the sensation of pressure as first the heel, then the ball of your foot makes contact with the ground. Be aware of your back foot starting to lift as your front foot makes contact.*

5 *Continue stepping in this attentive way, keeping your focus on the soles of your feet and noticing the actions of lifting, moving, placing. Breathe naturally and find your own pace.*

6 *When you reach the end of your walking space, pause and notice the experience of standing. Then turn—noticing the experience of turning—and walk back the other way. Continue walking back and forth for the period you have set for yourself.*

Meditative Practice

Awareness is not limited to the time we spend in formal meditation. We can bring the same open curiosity to any experience. In the forest monasteries of Thailand, sweeping the floor is an established meditative practice. Zen monks, meanwhile, have a communal practice called *soji*, in which everyone participates in cleaning the monastery. And the Vietnamese monk Thich Nhat Hanh advocates washing dishes as a form of workaday meditation.

Mindful chores

Consider a chore that you hate doing — say ironing. Have you ever found yourself going at it with a running commentary about how boring it is and what you are going to do when it is finished? When we do this, we just make the experience more difficult than it needs be. We make the present unpleasant. But treating chores as an opportunity for meditation can transform the way we feel about them.

Next time you have an unloved task to do, try approaching it with uncomplaining acceptance. Bring all your attention to what you are doing instead of wishing that it is over and done with.

Go slow

Slow down (what's a few more minutes anyway?) and treat this as a time to cultivate greater awareness. When you are doing a chore, do only the chore. Give it your full attention. Take note of as many of the senses as possible as you work — what you are seeing, hearing, smelling, touching. Or you may want to focus on only one sense: the sounds of sweeping, for example, or the tactile sensations as you fold laundry. If you notice yourself thinking how boring it is, you can simply label this "thinking" and return your attention to the task.

Give service

You may want to bring a quality of service to your chores, too. In Hindu ashrams and temples, there is a concept of *seva*, or selfless chores. So before you start a chore, you may want to "dedicate" it to your family or your housemates. Finding pleasure in the giving of service is a meditative practice in itself.

WASHING THE DISHES MEDITATION Even if you have

a dishwasher, washing dishes by hand can be a beautiful meditation exercise. One study at Florida State University found that people who focused on the full experience of washing dishes had reduced feelings of nervousness and increased feelings of inspiration, compared with a control group who did the chore in a mechanical way.

1 *Prepare to fill the sink with soapy water. Notice the experience of turning on the faucet and the sound of the water pouring out, and the feel and weight of the bottle of dishwashing detergent as you pick it up. Be aware of what you hear as the water hits the bottom of the bowl, and the sight of the bubbles forming.*

2 *Turn off the faucet, and pick up a dish, noticing how it feels in your hands. Place it in the water slowly, appreciating the warmth of the water. Take the sponge or brush in your hand, noticing how it feels, and use it to clean the front of the dish, then the back of the dish. Be aware of any sounds you hear as you do this.*

Choose a Chore

Try to do at least one chore a day with mindful awareness, even if it is a simple task such as making the bed or wiping the table. This is a good way to incorporate greater calm into your day and build your ability to focus.

3 *When the dish is clean, rinse it with the same level of attention, and then place it carefully on the side.*

4 *Pick up the next dish and bring the same full level of awareness to the process of washing the dish.*

5 *Be aware of your feelings— boredom, irritation, any faint disgust at unwashed dishes. Mark your thoughts, too: "Isn't this ridiculous?" or "Don't get why this is meditation." These are just feelings or thoughts—be aware of them and return your focus to the task in hand. When you are washing dishes, simply be washing dishes.*

6 *Try to maintain this mindful awareness for each dish. At the end of your dishwashing meditation, reflect on how you feel.*

Mindfulness of Eating

Prepared with care
Cooking can be a wonderful opportunity for mindfulness, because it involves sight, touch, smell, hearing, and taste. Try preparing your vegetables with full awareness of all five senses.

Mindfulness means being aware of the senses as we go about the day. This opens us up to the captivating experiences that are available in each moment. And eating is one of the great sensual joys of life. By focusing on the experience, we can turn eating into something richer and more exciting. This can also help us avoid negative habits, such as overeating or comfort eating.

We often eat while doing or thinking about something else. Or we eat because we are bored, upset, or just because the food is there. This leads to eating too much, or eating food that is not good for us, or even to eating food that we do not enjoy. However, bringing consciousness to mind can help to realign our eating habits. Begin by avoiding other activities when you eat. Turn off the TV, put your cell phone out of sight, make a point of sitting down. If you are eating alone, try using mealtimes as an opportunity for some silence.

A moment of thankfulness

It helps to have a moment of awareness before a meal, something akin to the Christian practice of saying grace. Spend a silent moment acknowledging that it is time to eat and giving your focus to the food in front of you. If you want, mentally express gratitude to those involved in bringing food to the plate—the grower and suppliers, and so on. You may also want to bring some small sense of ceremony to your mealtime by thoughtfully clearing and setting the table, or by placing flowers or candles on the table.

One Mouthful at a Time

Bring your awareness to each mouthful. Make a point of pausing between each forkful instead of loading it as you chew. Try to simply put your knife and fork (or sandwich) down, so you completely appreciate the food you are eating.

CHOCOLATE MEDITATION

A well-known mindfulness exercise involves eating a raisin, and it can be quite a revelation to discover the flood of sensations that we derive from one tiny morsel of food. This version of the exercise uses chocolate, but you can try it with any food that has an intense aroma and taste—a section of orange, a mint, an olive—or with a flavorful beverage, such as tea.

1 *Sit somewhere comfortable, with some chocolate before you. With your beginner's mind, take a moment to look at the chocolate, noticing the shape, the color. Pick it up, seeing if you can notice the intention to stretch out your arm before you move.*

2 *Hold the bar of chocolate in your hand, noticing how it feels. Snap a piece from the bar, noticing how this sounds. You may have the impulse to put it straight in your mouth; notice that this urge is there, but look at the piece of chocolate in your fingertips, examining it completely.*

Take One More

You can repeat the steps with another piece of chocolate, again noticing each moment and sensation. The same activity may seem very different a second time around.

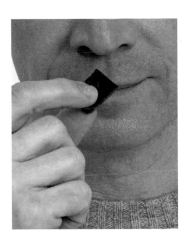

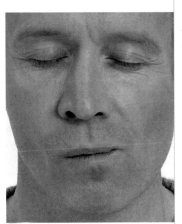

3 *Bring it slowly up and place it under your nose. Breathe in and experience the aroma. Notice if there is any salivation as you anticipate the taste—what does it feel like?*

4 *Now bring it to your mouth, being aware of how your mouth opens in readiness and how your hand automatically brings the chocolate to exactly the right place.*

5 *Place the chocolate on your tongue and notice how that feels— what tastes start to appear in the mouth, and where do they manifest as the chocolate melts?*

6 *Wait until the chocolate dissolves, then swallow it, noticing the movement of your tongue as you move the chocolate to the back of your throat.*

7 *Notice any lingering tastes in your mouth when you have swallowed the chocolate. Bring your awareness to how you are feeling. Do you think this tasting exercise has changed the way you experienced the chocolate?*

Meditation at Work

Step away
If you work on a computer, you can become oblivious to your surroundings, and to your body. Take regular breaks to stand up and breathe.

At work, we generally need to achieve and strive—we are in "doing mode." Meditation, meanwhile, is a process of cultivating presence, or "being" mode. Doing and being can be seen as opposites, but they are also mutually supportive. The issue many people have is that they are in "doing mode" too much. Meditation, and the related practice of mindfulness, can help to restore greater balance. Because these practices increase our ability to concentrate, they can improve our productivity. And they can help with clarity of mind and decision making.

One thing at a time

Multitasking is now known to be a fallacy. Each separate task ends up being done more slowly. A Dutch study found that interrupting your main task to, say, check emails was more disruptive than if you were interrupted by another person. In mindfulness practice, we learn to focus on one activity at a time, and this is a skill to carry through to the workplace. So turn off your email alert and cell phone and have specific times to check them instead of interrupting your task to respond instantly.

Take a cue

At intervals during your working day, use mindfulness to come back to the present moment. For example, you might choose always to wash your hands mindfully during rest-room breaks, or to take a deep breath whenever you sit down or stand up, or before answering a telephone call. For other micromeditations see page 112.

It's a good idea to go out at lunchtime. You could practice a short walking meditation (see pages 96–97), or sit on a bench and breathe for a few minutes.

Release the day

When you get home in the evening, find a way to put the busy-ness of the day behind you. Try taking off your shoes, and lying on the floor, with your arms above your head and your knees bent. Take a few moments to let your body release tension as you let the floor take your weight. Or make a point of getting changed into comfortable or clean clothing, taking a shower, or practicing meditation. Find a "coming-home" ritual that works for you.

COMMUTER'S NOTICING MEDITATION
Commuting is not all that good for you. A report by the UK's Royal Society for Public Health found that people who commute to work tend to be more stressed, and less satisfied with life in general. They also have a greater tendency to snack on unhealthy foods, and they get

1 *Take a seat if you can; otherwise do this standing. Spend a moment adjusting your posture so you are as comfortable as possible. Look ahead or slightly downward at a fixed point.*

2 *Take three or four conscious breaths. Now, without moving your head, find five things you can see: a sign on a train door, a flash of color on a fellow commuter's clothing, a mark on the floor.*

less exercise than other workers. But if you have to commute, meditation can at least help you make it a stiller, calmer experience. You can practice breathing, body sweeping, awareness of sound, or other meditations as you travel. This noticing exercise is good for when you feel too tense to turn the attention inward.

3 *Now find five things that you feel. The pressure of your feet on the floor, the weight of a bag on your shoulder, your sleeve rubbing against your wrist. Keep going until you have five.*

4 *Find five things you can hear: music leaking from someone's headphones, the rumble of the wheels. Don't get too caught up on the source of the sounds; just notice five different ones.*

5 *Repeat, but this time find only four things you can see, feel, hear.*

6 *Repeat again, finding only three things, then two things, then one thing. It doesn't matter if you repeat the same things.*

7 *When you reach one, go back to two, then three, four, and five. When you reach five, try spending some time resting in awareness, simply noticing whatever comes to your attention.*

Mindfulness in a Minute

Start afresh
*Make your waking moments count:
Instead of reaching for your phone,
make a point of attending to your
emotions and body sensations.*

It is very easy to be mindful for a moment or two, much harder to maintain an attitude of mindfulness for longer periods. Most of us are so used to going about our day on autopilot, only halfway aware of what we are doing, that it is difficult to remain in the moment. We need to use cues to remind ourselves to be more conscious, and we also need to support our wish to be more aware with formal meditation practice. Then, over time, mindfulness becomes an attitude that can infuse everything we do.

A wake-up call
Bring mindfulness into your morning routine to get the day off to a calm start.

Morning is a time when you are naturally alert, and your mind is generally clearer after a night's sleep. When you wake up, try taking three breaths with awareness before you get out of bed. Smile gently. Become aware of what you can feel—the touch of the sheets on your skin, the points of pressure where your body makes contact with the mattress and pillow, the heaviness where one leg rests on the other. Give yourself the gift of gently coming into these first moments without mentally running through a checklist of things to do.

Checking in
Make a point of checking in with yourself at regular intervals. Then, stop what you are doing and take a deep breath. Mentally scan through your body—are there any areas of discomfort, such as tight shoulders or a furrowed brow? As you breathe out, make a point of relaxing these areas as much as you are able. Notice your attitude of mind—are you straining or rushing, engaged or spaced out? It's fine to pause, allow yourself to come into the here and now, then resume what you are doing.

Take a cue

You could set an alert on your cell phone
as a reminder to check in. Or you can
attach your checking in to something you
do as a matter of course—perhaps
washing your hands, or making coffee.
You can also make a point of doing
certain activities with mindfulness—such
as opening a door, sitting down, or
picking up the telephone. Tying
mindfulness to these small actions is
a simple way to create pools of
stillness in the day.

Micromeditations

Micromeditations are short awareness or concentration exercises that you can do pretty much anywhere and at any time. They are a great way of bringing yourself into the moment, or of finding a little peace in the middle of a busy day.

Desk meditation

If you work at a desk or use one at home, clear a small section of it and place something here as a reminder of your meditation practice: a sculptural object, such as a shell, a single flower in a vase, or an arresting image. Use this as an object of focus for a minute to help steady your mind. Change the object from time to time.

Stop sign

Stop signs at pedestrian crossings or traffic lights can feel like a brake or an obstacle, but you can treat them as timely signals to pause instead. Bring your attention to what you can feel—the ground beneath your feet if you are walking—and take a moment to let go.

If you are driving, put your mind in neutral, rest your hands lightly on the wheel—and breathe. When the green light comes, set off with greater awareness.

Awareness walking

Bring mindfulness into any short walk that you do during the course of the day. If you have to walk to get to your car or reach the train station, use this time to come into your feet and ground yourself. Or try simply using this time to notice your surroundings—what can you see, smell, hear? Try looking upward at the sky at various points—it will change your perspective.

Animal Interaction

If you have a pet, this can be another opportunity to practice mindfulness. Petting animals is known to be inherently restful. So try letting go of doing anything else and spending a few minutes stroking your animal.

Find your pulse

Use the three middle fingers of one hand
on the pulse points of the wrist of your
other hand. You have to quieten yourself
to attend to the pulse, so it is a useful way
to come into the moment and also works
as a de-stressing technique. Count ten
pulses, or simply tune into the rhythm of
your pulse for a minute or two.

BUILDING
CONCENTRATION

Concentration practice means training the mind by giving it a specific object of focus. As we develop our ability to concentrate, we increase mental stamina and are better able to overcome distraction. Our objects of concentration can be internal—the most common is the breath, which is covered in chapter two—or they can be external. This chapter deals with external objects and covers the beautiful practices of mandala meditation, candle gazing, and the use of natural objects, such as a pebble or a flower. The chapter addresses the use of "aural" objects, such as the spiritual sound "Om," which is used as an aid to meditation in both the Tibetan and yogic traditions.

Objects of Concentration

Concentration and awareness are interlinked. We need to be aware of the breath in order to concentrate on it, and when we concentrate on the breath, we are able to become aware of it. In mindfulness or awareness practice, the ultimate aim is to rest in a state of open awareness or consciousness. In concentration practices, we bring all our attention to a single object of focus, or a single aspect of it, and hold our minds on it without wavering. This is known as one-pointed concentration, or one pointedness.

External objects

Many objects, internal or external, can be used for concentration practice. An external object is something that is tangible or concrete, such as a gemstone or a flower. Many spiritual traditions use an icon or artistic imagery; the beautiful Tibetan mandala (see page 115) can be used as a meditation focal point, as can the Hindu yantra.

Whichever object you choose, it should be something that is interesting enough to hold your attention. Your object does not necessarily have to be visual. It can be something tangible, such as a string of beads or a pebble in the hand; or aural, such as running water or the sound of your own chanting.

Internal objects

The most commonly used internal focus is the breath, but there are many others. For example, if you are part of a religious tradition, you might conjure up an image of a deity in your mind's eye. Alternatively, in yoga-based meditation, you might focus on the area between the eyebrows (the "third eye").

Trataka

In some concentration practices, including the yogic practice of trataka, you may shift between the external object and internal object. A candle flame is often used for this, because after gazing at it for some time, a residual image can be seen when you close your eyes—and in this way the flame becomes an internal object.

CANDLE FLAME MEDITATION

Candles are often used in worship and meditation. There is something about a flame that is inherently calming—perhaps it is something to do with the fact that the light and heat of a fire were so essential to our ancestors. This well-known meditation is best done in a draft-free room, because it is better if the flame is still instead of flickering.

1 *Dim the lights or close the drapes or blinds in your room. Place a candle on a table so it is at eye level, or slightly below it.*

2 *Sit about 3 feet (1 meter) away from the candle flame, and adopt a position that you can sustain comfortably. You should be directly in front of the flame so that you do not need to twist to look at it.*

3 *Look at the candle flame without blinking—try to gaze at an area of the flame instead of the candle itself. When you first start, you may not be able to do this for long, but gradually you will be able to build up the time. Be gentle with yourself, and do not cause yourself discomfort—that is not meditation.*

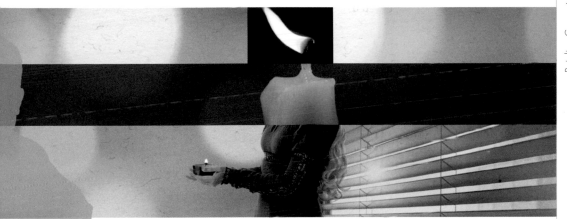

4 *Remain still as you gaze at the flame. At first, your mind may be scattered, but keep directing your attention back to the flame. You may find that your peripheral vision starts to fade as you focus on the flame. This can be a profoundly stilling and calming experience.*

5 *If your eyes start to water, then gently close them. You should be able to see an image of the candle imprinted behind your eyelids. Continue gazing at it, then when it fades, open your eyes and gaze at the candle again.*

6 *It any thoughts arise, try not to pay any attention to them but keep your concentrated attention on the flame.*

MANDALA MEDITATION

Mandalas are beautiful geometric designs that are used in Tibetan Buddhism as a tool for meditation. The word "mandala" means "circle" in Sanskrit, and mandalas are spiritually meaningful, circular designs. They are a picture or microcosm of the universe, not least because a circle has no beginning or

1 *Prop the mandala up on a table so that it is at eye level, or secure it to a wall.*

2 *Assume your chosen meditation position, and take a few deep breaths to relax your body.*

3 *Close your eyes gently for a few moments, then when you feel ready, open them. Focus on the centered point, keeping your gaze soft instead of fixed. And breathe naturally.*

Create a Focus

Any graphic representation can be used as a point for meditation. You could draw a cross and focus on the centered point. Or color in a round dot and look at that.

end. Meditating on a mandala is said to induce a sense of oneness or interconnectedness. You can create your own mandala, or find one that appeals to you—there are many available on the Internet.

4 *Look at the details of the mandala, letting your eye move systematically around it to take in the colors, shapes, and patterning.*

5 *Then close your eyes, keeping the image of the mandala in your mind. Are there blank parts, areas that you cannot recall? Open your eyes and look at the mandala again. Continue looking at the mandala, then closing your eyes to see what you retain of the image—with regular practice, you will get better at doing this.*

6 *At the end of the meditation, release your gaze from the mandala. Remain sitting for a few moments before you get up slowly.*

Using Natural Objects

Any natural object can be used for concentration practice. Natural things, such as shells or flowers or leaves or pinecones, are particularly good, because they are complex enough to hold your attention but small enough to be encompassed in their entirety by your gaze. And, of course, no flower, leaf, or shell is an exact copy of the next, so when we meditate on natural things, we are focusing on an object that is unique in the long history of the universe.

A world in microcosm

In our world, we are deluged with stimuli. We are subject to a constant torrent of data, of trivial things trying to draw our attention via screens, billboards, radios, storefronts. So it can be a relief—a kind of antidote to information overload—to look at a single object closely and mindfully.

A leaf is a particularly good object to choose, because we so rarely look at them individually. Usually we see them en masse, on a bush or a tree. And yet a single leaf is a wonderfully engaging thing. It is a machine for turning light into growth, carbon dioxide into breathable oxygen. And it contains within itself a branchlike structure that is like a stylized microcosm of the larger tree. So a leaf is at once something simple and complex.

Near and far

In most concentration practices, we usually look at an object that is small enough for us to take in. But you can experiment with distant objects. Try getting up high and looking at a particular point of a view. How long can you focus before your mind drifts?

Going deeper

When you first look at an object, you can be aware of yourself looking at it. But then, as you gaze at the object in all its detail, it can be useful to ask yourself "Who is looking?" Sometimes one can become aware that there is the act of looking, instead of a looker and an object. When you do this, the practice becomes an "insight" instead of a concentration exercise, and this shift of focus—away from what is materially there, toward the process that is occurring in a given moment—can be profoundly enlightening.

MEDITATION ON A LEAF

In concentration practices, as in awareness practices, we try to let go of our conceptualizing mind. What does this mean? It means examining the object and all its details like the dispassionate lens of a camera, but refraining from assessing the object in any way, or chattering about it in our mind. We simply observe the thing — in this case a leaf—just as it is.

1 *Place the leaf before you so you can see it without having to move your head. It should be on a cleared table or surface so there is nothing else in your sight line.*

2 *Close your eyes, and take a deep breath to relax into your meditation posture.*

3 *When your mind feels somewhat steady, open your eyes and gaze at the leaf. Look at it in its entirety—its shape and texture and color.*

A Changing Object

Keep a leaf or flower for a week and use this same object for your concentration practice each day. It will change as the process of decay begins, encouraging you to explore it afresh each day. And these changes help to remind us that all things are impermanent, that all things pass, which is a tenet of many religious and spiritual traditions.

4 *Let your gaze slide over the leaf, taking in the details—the subtle differences of color from one area to the next, the areas of dark and shade, depending on where the light hits it, any variations in texture, any holes or tears. Notice the edges, sharp or rounded, and the stem, if there is one.*

5 *If you become aware of tension in the eyelids or a sense of staring, gently close your eyes for a moment. Keep the quality of your observation gentle. Similarly, if you notice any thoughts arising, just gently guide your attention back to the object without a sense of judgment or self-criticism.*

Chanting & Mantras

Songs of praise

Certain prayers and parts of the Christian liturgy involve repeating set formulas, which is akin to chanting mantras in Buddhism and Hinduism.

Sound has long stood as a metaphor for a kind of creative spirituality. The stories of the indigenous peoples of Australia tell how the world was sung into existence by ancestral spirits. And, in the Judeo-Christian tradition, the cosmos begins when God speaks: "Let there be light!"

Repetitive sound has been used for thousands of years to create meditative states and commune with the gods. There is a tradition of chanting the same phrase or sound in many religious and spiritual traditions. In Christianity there is the affirming "Amen" or "Hallelujah" and set prayers, such as Hail Mary and the Lord's Prayer; in Judaism there is the Shema Yisrael; and in Islam the recitation of the 99 names of Allah.

Mantras

In Hinduism and Tibetan Buddhism, chanting mantras is a central feature of spiritual practice. The Sanskrit word "mantra" could be translated as "tool of the mind." Mantras are sacred words and phrases used as a way of communing with the divine, or of cultivating the qualities of particular deities. The mantra "Om" or "Aum" is seen as the most sacred mantra in Hinduism, Buddhism, Jainism, and Sikhism, because it stands for the resonance of the universe.

You can chant out loud, or repeat the mantra or sound silently in your mind. Either way, the mantra can function as an object of meditation and help develop one-pointed concentration.

The effect of a mantra

Scientific research has shown that chanting can reduce stress and anxiety. A study conducted by Imperial College London monitored the blood pressure and heart rate of Christian monks, and found it was at its lowest when they were practicing Gregorian chant.

Choosing a Mantra

You can use any word or phrase that resonates with you as a mantra: Calm, love, peace begins with me, or perhaps simply the sound "ahhhhh."

In some forms of meditation—including Transcendental Meditation™ and Primordial Sound Meditation™—you are given a personal mantra by your teacher.

OM CHANTING

Om—or Aum, as it is pronounced when chanting—is the most sacred of all mantras in Hinduism and Tibetan Buddhism. It is considered the heartbeat of the universe and of consciousness, and so chanting this mantra is said to

1 *Sit in your preferred meditation posture, and focus on the rising and falling motion of the belly as you breathe in and out. Close your eyes.*

2 *Inhale, and then on the out breath, slowly chant AUM (pronounced "ah-oo-m"), as if you are releasing it with your breath.*

- *Have your mouth open wide as you sound Aaaah*

- *Bring the lips into a round shape as you sound Ooooh*

- *Bring the lips together to sound Mmmmm.*

3 *Let your chant glide from one to another, making the sound as long as you can without effort. Feel the sound resonate through your body before it fades into silence.*

connect us to the cosmos and to oneness. It is commonly chanted at the start and end of some yoga and meditation classes, and many people find that the vibration of this sound has a calming and quietening effect on the mind and body.

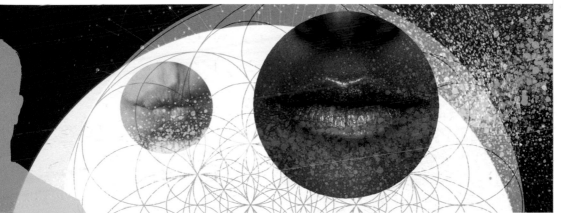

4 *Breathe in and repeat. Keep repeating the mantra for as long as you have chosen, directing your attention back to the sound whenever you find yourself distracted.*

The Meaning of Om

In Hinduism, Om, or Aum, represents Brahma, the supreme god, and is made up of three sounds:

A—representing the creation of the universe

U – representing the life of the universe

M—representing the destruction of the universe

When Aum fades away, the sound of silence represents enlightenment (beyond the universe).

THE SOHAM MANTRA
This is known as the "breath mantra" or "natural mantra," and is used in yoga or tantric meditation. The sound "so-ham" is an expression of the onomatopoeic sounds of the in breath ("soooo") and out breath (ham,

1 *Sit comfortably and close your eyes.*

2 *Bring your awareness to the passage of the breath in and out of your body at the nostrils. Notice the slight coldness of the air as it passes over the upper lip, and the barely perceptible sensation of the warmer out breath.*

3 *Gently tune into the sounds of your breathing. Then, when you feel steady, start to repeat the mantra silently to yourself— "sooooo" on the in breath and "hummmm" on the out breath.*

pronounced "hummmm"), and it is usually practiced silently. Because the sound of our breathing is one that is always with us, many people find this meditation easy to relate to. When you bring all your attention to this mantra, it is like the song of the breath.

HUMMMMM

4 *Synchronize the mantra with the natural rhythm of the breath. You may find that the exhalation starts to lengthen as you relax into the practice.*

5 *If you find your attention wandering, gently direct it back to the silent sound of the mantra.*

Posing a Question

In Sanskrit, "Soham" means "I am that" or "I am he," and is a way of aligning oneself with the universe or reality. The mantra is sometimes inverted so it is heard as "Hamsa." In Sanskrit, Hamsa poses the question: "Who am I?" And Soham answers: "I am that." However, in mantra practice, the meaning of the word is less significant than its sound.

USING A MALA

Buddhists, Hindus, and Sikhs often recite a mantra a set number of times, usually 108, because this is considered a sacred number. A mala—or string of prayer beads—is used to keep count, just as Catholics may use a rosary,

1 *Place your mala over the middle finger of your right hand, with the sumeru bead uppermost.*

2 *Rest your thumb on the small bead next to the sumeru bead. Then, once you have recited your mantra, gently push it away from you and slide your thumb onto the next bead.*

Choosing a Mala

The beads of a mala are always small and round, so they can move easily through your fingers. They are made from wood, bone, rudraksh seeds, sandalwood, or gemstones, and there is usually a small knot between each bead to make them easier to manipulate. Malas can be worn as a necklace or bracelet when you are not meditating. They then serve as a symbolic reminder of your intention to practice.

or members of the Russian Orthodox Church may use the beads known as "chetki." Malas usually have 108 beads plus a larger centered bead, known as a sumeru, bindu, or guru bead. Here's how to use a mala.

3 *Continue reciting your mantra, pushing the bead away each time. When you reach 108 recitations, you will be back at the sumeru bead. You can stop here, or turn the mala around and go in the opposite direction to complete another 108 recitations.*

Om Mani Padme Hum

A popular Tibetan Buddhist mantra often recited with a mala is the six-syllable Om Mani Padme Hum, associated with the enlightened being Avalokiteshvara, who represents compassion. The literal translation is "Praise to the jewel in the lotus," but its spiritual meaning goes far beyond this; all of the Buddha's teachings are said to be contained within this phrase. It is printed on prayer flags and on "prayer wheels" (see page 15)—and the Tibetans believe that spinning the prayer wheels has the same positive effect as reciting the mantra.

GOODWILL, COMPASSION & HEALING MEDITATIONS

When we meditate, we try to experience just what is. But it is also possible to use meditation to foster change—that is, as a tool for engendering positive emotional states. In this chapter, we look at exercises that are intended to cultivate goodwill or compassion, a greater sense of gratitude, or relaxation. Some, such as the mindfulness-based "surfing emotional waves" exercise, are healing ways to deal with difficult emotions. Others deal with the difficult shift involved in forgiveness. Many of these exercises have been scientifically investigated and found to have a positive effect. The final part of the chapter focuses on the Eastern concept of chi, or life force, and introduces traditional well-being exercises drawn from yogic philosophy or Taoism.

The Power of the Heart

Goodwill and compassion practices are intended to cultivate unconditional love and kindness. The best known of these practices is, in fact, called loving-kindness—*metta* in Pali—and is a teaching that we have inherited directly from the Buddha.

Testing the method

Research has shown that practicing goodwill can be an effective way to increase positive feelings and decrease negative ones. A famous study by the American psychologist Barbara Fredrickson found that practicing loving-kindness meditation for several weeks promoted positive emotions—which, in turn, generated a greater sense of purpose in life and even reduced physical symptoms of illness. Other research has found that practicing loving-kindness can increase empathy, encourage helpful behavior, and reduce self-criticism.

A shifting dynamic

In the practice of metta, we direct loving-kindness toward ourselves, our friends and family, our enemies, those we do not know, and ultimately to all beings—regardless of whether we deem them deserving or undeserving. Realizing that we can cultivate greater goodwill in ourselves can be a revelation. We may find that our feelings toward others, even individuals that we find difficult, shift considerably when we are able to wish them well. We may then act differently toward such people, perhaps being less defensive or critical. In turn, this may—possibly—change the way that they act toward us. So practicing goodwill can improve the dynamic of our relationships.

Helping ourselves

One thing that can help us to find goodwill or compassion is to remind ourselves that we are not alone in our feelings. We can feel isolated and alone, and it can be hard to credit that others suffer as we do. We all like to feel that we are somehow unique in our pain. But, of course, that is not so. Goodwill and compassion practices can reconnect us to a kind of fellow feeling, an imaginative empathy that may have the power to dissolve the boundaries between us.

Taking it farther

Loving-kindness is a formal meditation
practice, meaning that you sit and
practice it. But it is also something that
you can take into your daily life. Try to
silently direct the loving-kindness phrases
to people you pass on the street or on
your daily commute.

METTA BHAVANA, OR LOVING-KINDNESS This is the

traditional teaching, handed down from the Buddha, and still taught by meditation teachers. It involves sending goodwill first to ourselves, then to a benefactor, then a loved one, progressing to an acquaintance or neutral person, a person we dislike or find difficult, and eventually to a community and finally expanding it outward to all beings.

1 *Take care to find a position of comfort and ease. Sit upright and breathe deeply as you relax into your posture.*

2 *When you are ready to begin, create a mental picture of yourself smiling. Repeat these words silently to yourself, with care and gentleness:*

- *May I be safe*
- *May I be happy*
- *May I be healthy*
- *May I be free from suffering.*

3 *You may encounter resistance to these phrases, particularly when directing them to yourself. Do not struggle with it. As far as possible, continue to connect with the phrases and wish yourself well.*

Loving Yourself

In the traditional practice, you begin with yourself as an object of loving-kindness. However, sometimes it can feel painful or more difficult to wish yourself well than to direct your good wishes to others. If this is the case, change the order so that you start with the benefactor and loved ones, and then wish yourself well, before moving on to the neutral person.

4 *Keep saying the phrases to yourself for a period of time. When you feel ready, let the image of yourself fade and bring to mind someone who has helped and cared for you—a benefactor to whom you naturally feel grateful. This could be a beloved parent or grandparent, a teacher, or someone else who has guided you. Now, repeat the phrases as if saying them with meaning to this person:*

- *May you be safe*
- *May you be happy*
- *May you be healthy*
- *May you be free from suffering.*

5 *Next, imagine and say the phrases to a loved one: a sibling, a child, a dear friend. Choose someone you easily feel love for.*

Continued overleaf

6 *Then move on to a neutral person, someone you know but have no particular positive or negative feelings about. Perhaps someone at work, or a person you see regularly on your commute but have never spoken to. Imagine the person as best you can and direct the phrases to them.*

7 *Next, choose a person you dislike. In time, you may be able to send loving-kindness to someone you feel intense anger toward, but when you first start, it is better to pick someone who irritates or upsets you but who does not generate intense feelings of hatred. Be gentle on yourself. You may encounter more resistance when imagining this person. Keep the body relaxed and connect as best as you can to the phrases.*

8 *Now bring all these people before you: yourself, your benefactor, your loved one, your neutral person, and your difficult person. Direct the phrases to all of you at once:*

- *May we be safe*
- *May we be happy*
- *May we be healthy*
- *May we be free from suffering.*

9 *Then direct your good wishes from this group to all those in your vicinity, and let them radiate out to all those in your town or area, then your country, and finally the world—encompassing all sentient beings, people and animals— before bringing the meditation to a close.*

Sowing the Seeds

If you find metta practice challenging, as many people do, it is helpful to remember that you are laying a foundation for loving-kindness, or—as the Western teacher Jack Kornfield says—sowing its seeds in your heart. We cannot cultivate feelings through compulsion or by strained effort. We can only sit with the intention to send good wishes, and see what results come. It can take time and sustained practice for the seeds of our intention to come into flower.

TONGLEN

This is a Tibetan Buddhist practice, introduced to Tibet a thousand years ago by the Indian teacher Atisha. It is a beautiful practice in which you use pain and difficulty as a basis for generating feelings of love and compassion. Tonglen can help us to find tenderness and softness inside ourselves, creating a sense of peace. The word can be translated from the Tibetan as "giving and receiving."

1 *Sit on a cushion or chair, bringing the spine erect and then letting the body relax into this upright posture. Close your eyes or have them open, as you prefer.*

2 *Connect to a feeling of openness. You may find this easier if you first visualize a wide open space or perhaps the ocean. Rest in a sense of expansiveness for a few moments.*

3 *Bring your attention to your breath, letting it follow its natural path without trying to direct it in any way. As you breathe in, imagine you are breathing in darkness and heaviness; as you breathe out, imagine you are breathing out lightness and brightness. Continue breathing in darkness and breathing out light for a few minutes.*

4 *Bring to mind someone you know who is in pain or difficulty, someone you care for and would like to help. As you breathe in, imagine you are breathing in the darkness of this person's suffering. As you breathe out, imagine you are breathing out the brightness and lightness of compassion or love to this person. Continue breathing in their suffering and breathing out compassion.*

5 *Then expand your tonglen practice from your friend or loved one to all those who are suffering in the same way. Breathe in their suffering, and breathe out love and compassion, letting your compassion grow greater and greater. There is no limit to compassion.*

6 *Take a few moments to sit quietly to close the meditation.*

Gratitude Practice

Sending thanks
Writing a letter that tells someone why and how you appreciate him or her can be a powerful exercise for both writer and recipient.

Gratitude and awareness are complementary. This is because regular awareness practice can open up our minds to the many blessings we have in our lives, helping us to avoid taking them for granted. Conversely, when we take opportunities to express gratitude for the things in our lives, we become more aware and conscious.

So it is not surprising that most religious and spiritual systems have gratitude rituals. The Christian custom of saying grace before meals is one; then there is the Jewish concept of *hakarat hatov*, meaning "recognizing the good." And the fourteenth sura of the Koran proclaims:

"If you give thanks, I will give you more." Gratitude—and its counterpart, generosity—can help us to feel more connected to others. When we acknowledge what others give to us and what we give to them, everybody benefits; so it can be useful to practice a gratitude meditation, such as the one on pages 146–47.

Keeping a gratitude journal

Another popular way to cultivate appreciation is to keep a gratitude journal in which you record things you feel grateful for. The psychologist Robert A. Emmons has shown that this works best if you make a conscious effort to see the things that you write about as "gifts." When you sit down to write a gratitude journal, take a few moments to sit and breathe beforehand, so that it is heartfelt.

Letting gratitude spread

But gratitude need not be—and should not be—an action that you perform from time to time. It can become an attitude that informs all your waking hours. So, for example, you can make a habit of noticing the small services that others perform, and thanking them. If a kind driver lets you make a turn in front of them, be sure to give them a wave. If someone holds open a door, look them in the eye, smile, and say your "thank you" loud and clear. Make a point of articulating to others when they have done something you appreciate. Perhaps, if you feel thankful for the presence of some particular person, you could write them a letter saying why.

GRATITUDE MEDITATION

Even in difficult times, most of us have much to be grateful for, and this meditation helps you to remember this. If you notice a strong objection to feeling gratitude for a particular aspect of life, then leave this part of the meditation and move on. Sometimes our objections can surprise us and amount to an insight that we may need to reflect on.

1 *Spend a few moments settling yourself into a comfortable position, with your back upright but relaxed. Close your eyes and take a deep breath, in and out. Say inwardly to yourself: "I am thankful for this opportunity to be present" (you can amend the wording here and throughout, if you prefer).*

2 *Reflect on your senses. Say: "I am grateful for all that I can hear, smell, feel, touch in this moment." Next, reflect on your abilities. Say to yourself: "I am thankful for my ability to walk and move, to think and imagine, to feel and experience."*

3 *Reflect on your material possessions. Say to yourself: "I am thankful for all the gifts that I have in my life right now."*

Making Room

Sometimes when we try to reflect on life's gifts, feelings of lack or loss may surface. Try to acknowledge these with a sense of softness. The "difficult emotions" meditation (see page 164) may help.

4 *Reflect on the people who have been a positive presence in your life—your family or loved ones, friends, colleagues, teachers. Say to yourself: "I am thankful for all those who have come into my life."*

5 *Bring your awareness outward, imagining the vastness of the world in which we live. Take a moment to recognize the beauty of the planet. Say to yourself: "I am thankful for all the riches of the world I live in."*

6 *Rest for a few minutes in appreciation of the miracle of life. Say to yourself: "I am thankful for the gift of life." Let yourself enjoy this feeling of appreciation for all that you have before ending the meditation.*

The Power of Visualization

Visualization is an act of creative imagination in which we conceive the situation as if we were involved in it, instead of being only an observer. When we visualize, we let the image form from within our minds instead of mentally peering at it, as if on a screen.

Visualization features in many spiritual traditions, including the practice of yoga nidra, in which you are guided into a state of complete relaxation. It is also recommended as a de-stressing technique.

A trick of the mind

Many people believe they cannot visualize, yet they can. For a simple example of visualization, try imagining a lemon. Picture it before you, the sight of its bright yellow rind, and then imagine yourself picking it up, the texture and weight you can feel in your hand, cutting through to expose the cartwheel of the fruit inside. Now imagine the scent and the taste of that lemon. As you do this, notice what is happening in your mouth— is there saliva? A sense of anticipation? Just thinking about a lemon can have the same effect as handling a real lemon.

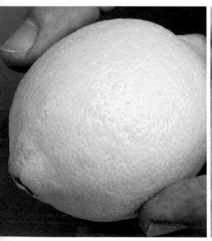

Scientific evidence

There is scientific evidence to suggest that the mental imagery used in visualization is interpreted in the same way by the brain as physical actions. One study at Ohio University found that people asked to visualize themselves performing exercises increased their muscle strength. In the study, a group of participants had their wrists strapped up so they could not move them, and were then instructed to imagine themselves flexing their muscles over a period of four weeks. At the end of that time, the wrist muscles were twice as strong as those of a control group.

Gentle effort

As with all meditations, the right level of effort is required. An attitude of force creates tension, making it difficult for the imagination to work creatively; too little effort, on the other hand, means there is not the concentration required and we are at the mercy of distraction. We need to focus, but with a degree of softness.

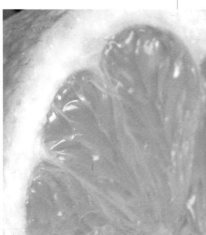

TROPICAL BEACH MEDITATION Visualizing a peaceful place,

where you feel safe and happy, is one way to counteract feelings of stress and so cultivate a sense of relaxation and calm. This exercise works best if you practice it regularly, but you can get positive results from doing it occasionally, too.

1 *Sit or lie down in any comfortable position. Close your eyes and take deep, slow, long breaths, letting your body release tension with each exhalation. If you want, do the body sweep (pages 64–67).*

2 *Now imagine yourself walking along a pathway. You come to a sandy beach and look at the glittering, turquoise ocean in front of you. You can hear the gentle sigh of the waves as they break on the shore.*

3 *Feel the soft warm sand beneath your bare toes as you walk toward the water with the sun caressing your face. As you come closer, you smell the salty aroma of the ocean; perhaps you can taste it on your lips.*

4 Walk into the surf, feeling the coolness of the waves as they wash over your feet and ankles. Perhaps you go farther, letting yourself be submerged by the water, as you lift your face up to the sun.

5 When you feel refreshed, leave the water and walk back up the sandy beach. Find a place in the dunes to lie down and rest, feeling the warmth of the sun on your body and the softness of the sand supporting you. You are able to let go and relax completely in this beautiful place.

6 When it is time to go, get up and slowly trace your way back to the pathway. Walk away from the beach—knowing you can come back here at any time. Slowly bring your awareness back to your present surroundings and open your eyes. Try to keep this same sense of softness and relaxation with you.

BEST POSSIBLE SELF

In this exercise, you visualize yourself at some point in the future, having achieved a dream or successfully reached a milestone. A study by researchers at Maastricht University in the Netherlands found that

1 *Assume a comfortable meditation posture and take a few slow, deep breaths, letting your body settle and relax with each out breath.*

2 *With your eyes closed, imagine a time in the future—it could be next week, next month, next year, or in a few years' time.*

3 *Imagine that everything has gone as well as possible in your life. Visualize yourself at this time, happy and fulfilled or successful in a way that is meaningful to you. If you feel resistant to visualizing success, remember how easy it was to visualize that lemon—it's exactly the same process. You should be achieving some realistic aim—perhaps meeting a partner, starting a family, getting a desired promotion or qualification, being in top physical health—instead of an impossible fantasy, such as walking on Mars.*

visualizing one's best possible self for five minutes a day over two weeks boosted mood and increased a sense of optimism. Other studies have found that it enhances psychological well-being and can improve motivation.

4 *Sketch in as much detail as possible. If you are visualizing yourself running your own company, for example, think about your role, who you would be working with, where you would be. If you are imagining yourself as fit and healthy, picture yourself at the gym or crossing the finish line in a marathon.*

Put Pen to Paper

When you have done this meditation, take some time to write about this brighter future. This helps to clarify your goals and naturally shift your priorities in alignment with them. Revisit your notes from time to time to check whether you are acting in ways that support your long-term aims.

Learning to Let Go

The burn of anger

We can become attached to the hot coal of our anger, and to thoughts of revenge. This keeps us tied to the pain of our past.

All meditation involves letting go. On a purely physical level, there is the regular, continuous release of the breath. When we exhale, we are attentively and purposely letting go of one breath in order to make space for the next.

That respiratory process, taking place over and over again in our lungs, is a kind of picture of what goes on in our minds. When we notice a random thought, we aim to let it go instead of becoming carried away with it. When we notice ourselves wishing for our experience to be different, we remind ourselves to let that go, too. Holding on would be as pointless and unproductive as holding the breath.

The hot coal

A vivid Buddhist story illustrates the concept of letting go of difficult emotion—in this instance, anger. It is said that anger is like a hot coal that we pick up to throw at the person who has angered us. But, of course, the only person who is certain to be burned by the coal is the one who throws it.

The point is that clinging onto emotions never helps. Nor, for that matter, does it help to push emotions away, since that is also a fruitless effort. It is an enervating conflict with the self. Letting go means coming into one's present experience just as it is. And so we let go of fantasies about the future (wishful thinking), and of worries about what might happen. We let go of regrets about things that have happened, and of a longing to return to the past (nostalgia). We let go of all our desire for things to be different, or for ourselves to be different—to be calmer, happier, nicer, richer, more successful.

This is certainly not easy to achieve. But it is worth the attempt. And it is worth persevering, even though we will fail many times in the attempt and have to start again. Don't worry about not managing to let go—let go of that, too.

FORGIVENESS MEDITATION

When we hold on to grudges and old resentment we bind ourselves to the past, which prevents us from appreciating and experiencing the present. Sometimes we feel remorse at our own actions, and this, too, can keep us from embracing the here and now.

1 *Sit comfortably, taking some deep breaths and relaxing into your posture. Bring your awareness to your heart area. Become aware of how it feels right now, without judging the sensations that you feel. Is there heaviness or numbness? A sense of something that is closed up, or else unprotected?*

2 *Turn your attention to a person toward whom you feel resentment or anger—someone who has harmed you in some way. As you bring this person and the offense to mind, see if you can notice a sense of holding onto the pain.*

3 *Try whispering the person's name and silently repeat the words: "For any pain you have caused me, I forgive you." If you are unable to feel a wholehearted sense of forgiveness, you can amend these words to say: "I forgive you as far as I am able to do so at this moment."*

Forgiving oneself and forgiving others is not the same as condoning harmful behavior, nor does it mean you need to maintain a relationship with someone who has harmed you. Forgiveness is a way of allowing for space in your heart, so you can move on from the pain of the past.

4 *Let the meaning of the words work their way into your heart. Forgiveness cannot be forced; all you are doing here is opening up to the possibility of forgiveness, like a door ajar.*

5 *Now think of someone that you want to seek forgiveness from. As vividly as you can, bring to mind this person or the situation in which the pain was caused. Let your awareness encompass any feelings or sensations you may experience in the heart area or elsewhere in the body.*

Continued overleaf

Accessing the Heart

Practicing the forgiveness meditation can be a good preparation for loving-kindness meditation. When we let go of resentment, this helps to open the heart and makes the generation of goodwill toward others easier.

6 *Silently or out loud, softly whisper the person's name and say: "For any harm I have caused you, I ask for your forgiveness. Please forgive me." Repeat these words softly and gently. Again, you may notice a shift or change within yourself, or else a feeling of numbness or resistance. Place your hand on the heart area as you repeat the words if you find that helps you to soften.*

7 *Now move on to cultivating a sense of forgiveness toward yourself, for all the ways that you have harmed or wounded yourself—through harsh self-criticism or unwise actions.*

8 *Silently or out loud, say: "For any harm I have caused myself, I forgive myself." Face any sense of regret or shame with gentleness. Remember that all you are doing is setting the intention to forgive yourself; let the feelings come in their own time.*

Release Expectation

You may find that you do not feel any sense of letting go when you do the forgiveness exercise, but in time the words may resonate more deeply. Sometimes the long-held pain of old offenses may resurface. Be gentle with yourself and find ways to support and hold yourself if this happens, or seek support from others. Sometimes you may want to explore your feelings in counseling or therapy.

CUTTING TIES MEDITATION

This visualization can be helpful if a relationship has ended and you need to cut the emotional ties that bind you to it. It can also be useful for helping yourself find a sense of detachment and separateness from harmful relationships that are in the past but still affect you. Letting go of old ties can take time, so you may like to practice the meditation every day for a couple of weeks.

1 *Sit in a upright meditation position. Take some slow, deep breaths, letting your body relax into your posture with each out breath.*

2 *Bring to mind the person who you want to detach from. Imagine that they are sitting in front of you. Try to visualize them in as much detail as possible.*

3 *Imagine a golden ribbon that circles you without touching you. Now imagine that it unfurls and—moving n the opposite direction—winds around the other person. It now forms a figure-eight, and you are each sitting in one encircling half of it.*

4 Visualize this ribbon continuing to move in its figure-eight, encompassing you to the person in front of you. If it feels right and appropriate — it may not do — you might want to thank the person for the presence in your life, or tell him or her that it is time to cut the ties that bind you.

5 Now imagine that you have a large pair of scissors in your hand. When you feel ready and the image is clear, take the scissors and cut through the center of the figure-eight.

6 Let the ribbon continue winding around each of you — now in separate circles. Then gradually let the image of this person fade away. Take a few moments to sit and breathe before releasing the image of the ribbon.

HO'OPONOPONO

This is a traditional Hawaiian practice of reconciliation that can be a very healing way of making things right or coming to terms with the past. It involves saying four key phrases, either silently or out loud. Ho'oponopono can feel particularly powerful if you practice it in a beautiful environment in which you can let yourself be touched by the expanse and wonder of the world.

1 *Sit or stand in a comfortable posture. Take a few deep, slow breaths, letting your body relax. You can do this with your eyes open and resting on some object of beauty; half-open and resting on the floor in front of you; or closed.*

2 *Say the following phrases:*

"I'm sorry."

This is taking responsibility for your experience and the way that you feel. It doesn't matter what you are saying sorry for—we all have things that we regret. All that matters is that you express these words of repentance.

"Please forgive me."

Say these words. Sometimes we can struggle to ask for forgiveness, perhaps because we have feelings of shame or unworthiness, perhaps because we do not want to accept our failings. Express these words with meaning, whether they are attached to a specific event or not.

"Thank you."

Speak those words of gratitude. Feeling thankful can sometimes be a challenge, so if these words do not resonate with you at first, that's fine.

"I love you."

Finally, say the words of love. Again, the words do not need to be directed at anyone or anything in particular. You may feel a sense of love for a particular person, or for the universe in general. Or you may struggle to feel a sense of love. Whatever you feel is fine.

3 *Keep repeating the phrases with meaning and care, until you feel some sense of release or shifting.*

Meditation & Difficult Emotions

People sometimes think that meditation can turn them into a calm, Zen-like person. But however far you go with meditation, you will still fall prey to intense and unpleasant emotions—anger, shame, jealousy, disappointment, grief. But meditation can provide a way of working with these emotions. Instead of trying to deny their existence or, conversely, justify it, we can simply accept emotions as one more state that arises, is present, and fades away. We can then, hopefully, carry this awareness into our daily lives, and respond more skillfully to emotions when they arise.

An emotional release

Meditation involves opening up to our experience. This can create a kind of space into which repressed emotions can flow, like groundwater flowing into a rock fissure. It's possible you may feel a surge of, say, grief or rage in the middle of your meditation practice, sometimes for no apparent reason. There may be physical sensations, too, such as restlessness or nausea. This is normal and the task in meditation is not to make the emotions go away, but to notice them and explore them. This can be an intense experience, and one that can provide profound insights. Sometimes it may be appropriate to seek help, perhaps from an experienced therapist or trusted meditation teacher.

Two arrows

There are two main aspects to our emotions—the feeling itself, and the story that is attached to it. "The story" is the way the mind interprets and narrates the feelings. In meditation, we try to explore the pure sensations of feeling without getting caught up in storytelling. The Buddha addressed these dual aspects of emotion in an analogy known as "the two arrows." The first arrow is the suffering that all of us encounter in life—disappointment, loss, physical pain. It cannot be dodged because it is part of human experience, but if we lament our pain, complain how unfair it is, try to pretend it doesn't exist, then we only increase our suffering. This needless pain is the second arrow. In meditation, we learn to face the reality of the first arrow, thereby avoiding the second.

SURFING EMOTIONAL WAVES

Emotions come and go like the tides. We cannot stop them altogether, but we can learn to ride them out. When you notice the ocean swell of a difficult emotion, try this technique. It's useful in daily life as well as in meditation practice.

1 *Find some steadiness in your posture. If you are sitting on a chair, make sure your legs are uncrossed and both feet are flat on the floor.*

2 *Bring your awareness to the sensations you are feeling in your body—tightness in your belly, pressure in your throat, tension in your jaw or shoulders, a fizzing sensation in your head.*

3 *Give a name to the emotion that you associate with these feelings—anxiety, worry, grief, sadness, rage. If this feels difficult, you can simply name them "feeling."*

4 *See if you can cultivate a feeling of softness and openness toward these feelings, allowing space for them to be present. This is a hard thing to achieve, and it involves cultivating an awareness that you are separate from the emotion. Your emotion is not you, and you are neither passively engulfed by it nor actively whipping it up.*

Take good care of yourself in the aftermath of this exercise. Keep warm, have a glass of water if you need it, go for a walk.

5 Sometimes the feeling may move elsewhere in the body or dissipate altogether, like a wave breaking on the shore. Or else it may grow bigger and more intense—like a strong tidal surge. Stay with the feeling as it moves through you or perhaps takes different forms.

6 Remember that you are simply noticing the physicality and energy of this emotion. If thoughts or stories intrude, it may help to repeat: "I can feel this feeling without getting carried away" or simply "It's okay."

7 When the feeling passes, stay sitting for a time, perhaps attending to the breath, or perhaps simply experiencing the moment.

Working with Energy

Many Eastern philosophies are based on the idea of spiritual energy or animating force. It is known as *chi* in China, *ki* in Japan, and *prana* in India. The concept of chi, or life force, is central to many Eastern forms of healing and physical arts—for example, acupuncture, qigong, tai chi, aikido, reiki healing, and yoga.

The flow of chi

Most philosophies hold that energy should flow freely around the body, and that when energy is blocked or depleted, physical and mental imbalances can occur. You can balance and increase the flow of chi around the body in various ways—through breathing exercises, through physical exercises, or through body work. Meditation can be a way of tuning into the energy in and around the body, and using the mind to work with chi. Even if you are not consciously working with energy, you may undergo experiences that can be usefully explained by the idea of energy or spirit.

The dantians and chakras

Each of the various philosophies that acknowledges chi has its own way of mapping the energy flow around the body. In Taoist-derived practices, such as tai chi or Chinese medicine, chi is held to flow through "meridians." These follow different routes to the *nadis* used in Hindu-based practices.

In Taoism, there are said to be three main centers of energy in the body—the lower, middle, and upper dantian, which are in the lower belly, the heart area, and the forehead. Dantians are seen as storehouses of energy—somewhat like batteries. In Hinduism, there are seven energy centers, known as chakras (meaning "wheels"). These are seen as doorways or vortices through which energy can flow in and out of the body, and be transformed from the physical or emotional plane to the spiritual. You could say that the dantians roughly correspond to three of the chakras. However, it is better to see them as different systems and work with one or the other.

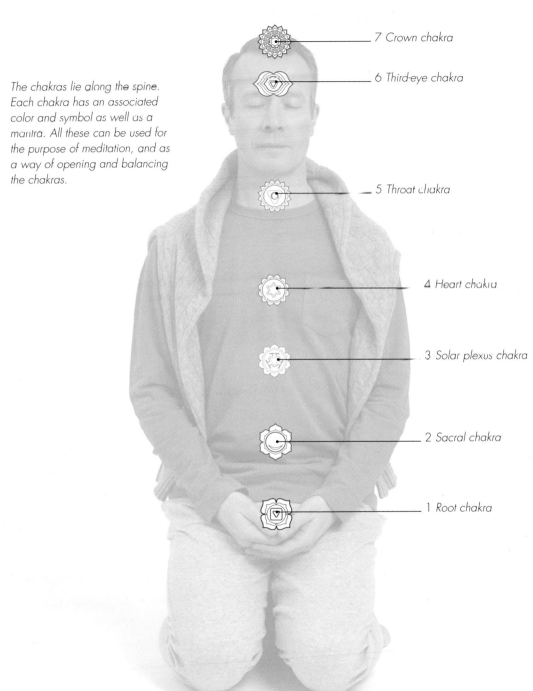

The chakras lie along the spine. Each chakra has an associated color and symbol as well as a mantra. All these can be used for the purpose of meditation, and as a way of opening and balancing the chakras.

7 Crown chakra

6 Third-eye chakra

5 Throat chakra

4 Heart chakra

3 Solar plexus chakra

2 Sacral chakra

1 Root chakra

OPENING THE HEART

In this meditation, you direct your attention to the heart chakra. It is the seat of our emotions, encompassing our love for others and for ourselves as well as our love for the universe. Of the seven chakras, the heart chakra is the centered one and, therefore, a bridge between the lower and higher chakras.

1 *Sit on the floor or on a chair with your spine upright and your shoulders relaxed. Become aware of the breath, focusing on the chest area and noticing how it expands and contracts with the breath.*

2 *Take deep slow breaths, using the out breath to help you relax into the meditation.*

3 *As you continue to breathe, visualize the glow of an emerald green light that emanates from the heart. It is often imagined as a spinning spiral of light, but you can visualize something simpler, such as a circle or sphere, if you find that easier.*

This visualization can be a useful prelude to metta or the forgiveness meditation, particularly if you find it difficult to connect with words of love or forgiveness. You can work with the other chakras in the same way, using their individual colors.

4 Know that this light is the embodiment of love and compassion. Let this glowing light radiate outward, growing larger and larger until it covers the chest, releasing any tension or tightness, any sorrow or emotional pain.

5 Continue imagining this sphere of light getting larger and larger until it covers the rest of your body—your arms and hands, your head and feet. Rest in this beautiful emerald green light that emanates from your heart center.

6 Continue to breathe and visualize this green light for some minutes.

7 At the end of the meditation, gently bring your attention back to the body and the sensations of the breath at the chest. Become aware of the boundaries of your body—your fingers and toes, the points where your body is in contact with the floor or chair. Slowly open your eyes and remain sitting for a few moments as you take in your surroundings.

TAOIST TREE MEDITATION

In Taoism, it is held that trees are able to meditate, and do so unceasingly. Taoist practitioners cite trees' stillness, their immovable rootedness in the earth, and their transformative power—trees, after all, take carbon dioxide, the waste product of respiration, and turn it into life-giving oxygen. In this exercise, you use visualization to evoke a treelike groundedness.

1 *Sit in a comfortable meditation position, with your spine upright. Make sure you have a solid, stable base to your posture.*

2 *Quieten yourself by bringing your attention to your breathing, attending to the sensations of the belly rising and falling.*

3 *Breathe into the lower dantian, which is a few inches below your navel and inside your body. Breathe into this area, feeling it expand and contract as you breathe in and out.*

4 *Now, when you breathe out, imagine that your breath moves down from the dantian and through the base of your body into the earth below you, visualizing yourself as a tree and your breath as roots pushing down.*

Out in the Open

You can do this exercise while sitting next to a tree, or perhaps with your back to it. Or try standing with your palms resting near or on the trunk of a tree, and imagine that you are drawing energy from it as you breathe in and sending that energy down into the earth with your out breath.

5 *As you breathe in, imagine that you are drawing energy and nutrients up from the earth through your roots and into your dantian. Let this breath come up through the spine, as if it were your trunk, and through the rest of the body—like the branches of a tree.*

6 *Continue breathing in and out, sending roots down into the earth with your out breath and drawing up the healing grounding energy of the earth with your in breath, imagining yourself as a tree— grounded and strong.*

7 *At the end of the meditation, release the mental image of a tree and bring yourself back to your surroundings. Remain sitting for a few moments.*

The Inner Smile

This profound Taoist practice involves using the positive energy of a smile to cultivate healing joy and to encourage the flow of chi (or life force) through the body. It is the best-known exercise within "neidan gong," the Taoist idea of "inner alchemy," and it is often practiced in conjunction with qigong.

Smiling and mood

It is a known fact that smiling has a positive effect on mood. Modern research has shown that smiling reduces levels of the stress hormone cortisol in the body, and also stimulates the production of endorphins, the feel-good hormones. This meditation is an invitation to offer the gift of a smile to your inner organs; Taoists say that if you smile at your organs, they will smile back at you.

In the inner smile, you start by bringing your mouth into a gentle smile with the mouth closed and let that smile travel to your eyes. You experience the warmth and benevolence of the smile and let it suffuse your head and face. From there, you imagine the energy of the smile flowing down to different parts of the body.

The flow of chi

According to Taoism, focusing radiant smiling energy on a particular area of the body helps to release blocked energy and promote the flow of healing chi there. The Taoists believe that different emotions are associated with the main organs, and practicing this meditation can sometimes have a transformative effect on negative feelings, such as anger or bitterness. You may also find it harder to focus on some organs or parts of the body than others. Be gentle with yourself, and try to avoid the tendency to judge.

Know your anatomy

It's makes sense to have a rough anatomical idea of where particular organs are located before you begin this meditation, but you don't need to be too precise—simply direct the smiling energy to roughly the right area. You may be able to connect with a sense of what is happening inside the body, and sense each organ, or you may not. Over time, this practice will help to deepen your awareness of the inner body.

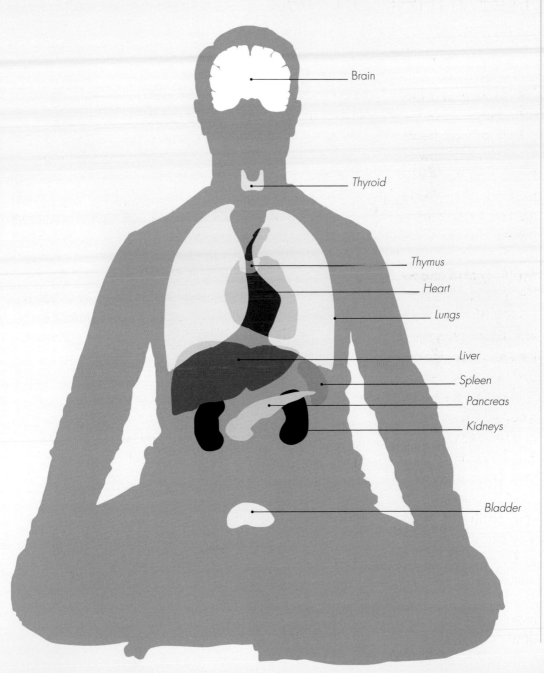

Brain

Thyroid

Thymus

Heart

Lungs

Liver

Spleen

Pancreas

Kidneys

Bladder

PRACTICING THE INNER SMILE

The inner smile is a beautiful practice that brings healing to the body and encourages us to cultivate self-kindness and gentleness. As you go through the steps of this exercise, try to remain connected with the loving compassionate energy of a gentle smile. If you find yourself becoming

1 *Sit comfortably upright. Rest the tip of your tongue on the hard area behind your front teeth. Take a few moments to breathe deeply into the belly and slowly release any tension here.*

2 *Bring your mouth into a gentle smile. Let the smile travel up your face so that it encompasses your eyes as well as your mouth.*

3 *Spend a few moments letting this inner smile flow freely here and around your whole head and face, so that it reaches the back of the skull, the ears, the back of the eyes, the jaw—until every part and the spaces in between are filled with smiling energy.*

tense or judgmental at any point, then simply pause and breathe before returning to your smile. As with all meditations, finding the right level of concentration is a subtle art. We need to find harmony between effort and acceptance, and this comes more easily with practice.

4 *Let the energy cascade down your neck and throat to the thyroid, just behind the Adam's apple. You may experience a sense of warmth or release here. When you are ready, direct the flow toward the thymus, behind your breastbone, and let it permeate here.*

5 *Now imagine this warm smiling energy flowing farther, filling your heart with love and happiness. Linger as long as you want here—mentally focusing on this organ that sends healing energy to every part of the body. Feel your heart become more open and relaxed as the smiling energy continues to flow into and around it.*

Continued overleaf

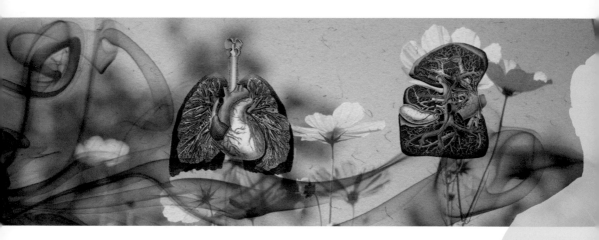

6 When you are ready, let this smiling energy radiate out from your heart, bringing healing joy to the lungs. Notice yourself breathing more freely.

7 Now let the smile energy radiate from your heart toward the spleen, on the left of the body, within the rib cage, and then moving across to the pancreas, which is roughly in the center.

8 Bring your focus back to your heart and direct the smile energy to your liver on your right side, just beneath the ribs, then to the kidneys, which are at the back of the body, on each side of the spine and just below the rib cage. Now direct this loving smile energy to the bladder, just above and behind the pelvis, and then to the genitals.

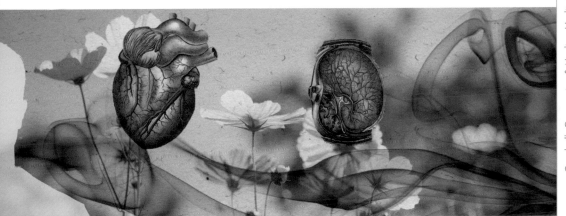

9 Bring your inner smile to the digestive system. Bringing your focus back to the mouth area allows for saliva to accumulate. Swallow it down, and as it travels down the esophagus, imagine your smiling energy traveling with it, down into the stomach and intestines, then on to the colon and rectum.

10 Return to your eyes and mouth, and bring the smiling energy down the spine, vertebra by vertebra, to the base. Feel your spine fill with happiness and warmth as you do this, then let the smiling energy radiate out through the sacrum and pelvis.

11 To finish, bring the flow of smiling energy to the area behind and just below the navel—this is an important storehouse of chi in the body. Spend a few moments storing your smile energy before you end the meditation.

A BROADER,
DEEPER PRACTICE

The natural consequence of meditation is increased awareness. This often leads, in turn, to a more ethical attitude, as you gain a clearer and more far-sighted picture of how you live in the world. Most spiritual traditions, in most ages, have recognized the connection between introspection and right living. This chapter introduces you to the concept of "contemplative meditation," and suggests some ways to practice it. The exercises are drawn from a range of spiritual traditions, including Hinduism and Christianity, and some can be adapted to suit your own worldview. The chapter also looks at ways that you can bring the benefits of your practice to your relationships through mindful communication and partner meditation, and offers practical advice on sharing meditation with your children.

Meditation & Ethical Living

Traditionally, meditation has always been part of a wider system that encompasses ethical living. In classical yoga, the eightfold path includes meditation, breath control, physical postures, and a set of ethical guidelines known as the *yamas* (restraints, or how not to act) and *niyamas* (observances, or ethical ways to act). Modern secular meditation and yoga programs, as practiced in the West, have largely abandoned this ancient connection with ethical living. In many ways, this is a pity, because meditation can be about something wider and deeper than the self and one's own issues.

Hand in hand

Meditation and ethics can be mutually supportive of each other. Research suggests that people who meditate become more inclined to behave altruistically—even in very small ways. One study found, for example, that participants who had undergone an eight-week course in mindfulness were twice as likely to give up their seat to someone who needed it. This is perhaps a kindly effect of the greater awareness that meditative practices can bring.

By carrying through to our daily life the insights we discover in meditation, we create greater continuity between our practice and our life. When we meditate, we witness our thoughts, feelings, and emotions without getting caught up in them. This means that selfish or grasping mental states are less likely to direct our actions in the other parts of our daily life. Once that occurs, it is easier for us to cultivate the positive mental states we need for meditation. Thus, by acting in ways that are unselfish and for the good of others, we create an emotional milieu that can ultimately benefit ourselves; living in an ethical way can help to strengthen and deepen our meditation practice.

Precepts and Yamas

Central to Buddhist teachings are the five "precepts": refraining from harming living things; stealing or taking what has not been freely given; sexual misconduct; lying or gossip; and taking intoxicating substances. The precepts are derived from the Hindu concept of yamas, a set of desirable qualities defined as: nonviolence (ahimsa), truthfulness (satya), nonstealing (asteya), nonexcess (brahmacharya, often translated as chastity), nongreed (aparigraha).

THE FIVE PRECEPTS MEDITATION

The five precepts are principles or training guidelines that all Buddhists willingly embrace. To all of us, whatever our religion, they can be useful encouragements for living well. But if you have strong religious convictions of your own, you may prefer to amend the wording to something that suits your outlook—similar guidelines can be found in all the major religions. Practice this meditation each morning to set the tone for your day.

1 *Get into a comfortable meditation position and close your eyes. Spend a few moments concentrating on the breath as you experience it at the nostrils, chest, or belly—wherever it is most apparent.*

2 *Reflect on the first precept. Abstaining from taking life. It's a fundamental moral principle that everyone has the right to life, and in Buddhism this extends to animals as well. The principle includes the avoidance of physical harm or injury to any other being. This precept helps to cultivate love and compassion.*

3 *Reflect on the second precept. Abstaining from taking what is not given. This means not stealing, of course, but also refraining from taking anything that has not been freely and explicitly granted. So taking pens from work would count as an infringement of the precept, as would eating someone else's stash of chocolate. This precept helps to cultivate generosity.*

4 *Reflect on the third precept. Abstaining from sexual misconduct. This means not only being faithful to a partner, but also not playing with the feelings of others or causing harm in relation to sex. This precept helps to cultivate self-control.*

5 *Reflect on the fourth precept. Abstaining from false speech. Lying and gossiping are characterized as false speech, as are idle talk and rudeness. This precept helps to cultivate truthfulness and integrity.*

6 *Reflect on the fifth precept. Abstaining from intoxication. Intoxicants are any substances that cloud the mind. As well as abstaining from alcohol and drugs, one should avoid caffeinated beverages, especially before meditation practice.*

MINDFUL SPEECH

Cultivating mindful speech is one of the simplest ways to introduce a more ethical attitude into your daily life. Speaking, after all, is a form of action—a crucial and singularly powerful one—because it is easy to do real harm or achieve great good with a few words. Try spending a day following these guidelines.

1 Be honest

When you speak, be clear that what you say is truthful and not intended to deceive in any way. This includes being factual, as well as making sure that you don't neglect to speak the whole truth.

2 Promote harmony

Sometimes you may need to say something that others don't like, of course, but avoid speaking to others in a way that will probably cause harm or division. Make a point of not speaking about other people in a negative way or sharing private information about them. Gossip is not mindful.

3 Choose your words carefully

Think about what you want to say before you voice it, choosing words that are clear or kind. Avoid rude or abusive language. Swearing and harsh language is another form of speech that is not mindful. Choosing the right time to say something is also important.

4 Make it worthwhile

Much of the time we speak for the sake of it. Letting yourself get comfortable with silence is a key part of mindful speech. Don't talk for the sake of it.

5 Extend your view of speech to written speech

If you intend to post on social media, run through the above guidelines before you do so.

Silence and Intention

It can be illuminating to realize how difficult it is to maintain mindful speech—even over the course of a short conversation. It is helpful to start the day with a period of silent meditation to settle the mind. Try to think about your intention before you speak. This helps you to bring greater awareness to your speech and also to inculcate the habit of thoughts that are more conducive to meditation. Mindful listening is a related practice—see pages 208–9.

Contemplative Practices

Contemplation is deep, reflective thought. It differs from concentration practices in that, with contemplation, the object of our focus is not narrow and intense. Instead, contemplation is openended and expansive—allowing for unplanned possibilities and unexpected understanding to emerge.

The ultimate aim of many contemplation practices is to transcend thought and come to rest in a point beyond consciousness. At this point, a person can sometimes become aware of the spacious nature of all things and comprehend that, on the deepest level, there is no distinction between the object of contemplation and oneself.

The oneness of things

This intention may sound esoteric or even downright wacky, but the oneness of things is supported by, or paralleled by, the facts of physics. Everything that we perceive as solid and separate in the normal run of things is nothing more or less than a shimmering mass of atoms, each one a tiny galaxy of particles. And everything we see and know—ourselves and others, living things and inanimate things—is formed of atoms that were born of stars billions of years ago.

This is what the astronomer Carl Sagan meant when he remarked that in order to make an apple pie from scratch, one must first invent the universe. He was talking about astrophysics, but meditation masters from the Buddha to the twentieth-century sage Ramana Maharshi (see page 190) seem to have arrived at analogous truths entirely intuitively. They have seen that there is no substantial difference between their own consciousness and everything that lies outside of it.

The briefest moment of such a revelation can be a profound experience. It can also sometimes be disconcerting. If you experience emotions, such as fear or anxiety, while doing this practice, you can view these feelings in the same way as any other phenomena—as temporary events that can be observed and then let go. However, for this reason, contemplative meditations are best attempted when you have already achieved a degree of steadiness of mind through concentration and awareness practice.

WHO AM I? MEDITATION

The Indian spiritual sage Ramana Maharshi taught self-inquiry as a way of uncovering our true nature. His teaching encourages us to ask: "What does 'I' mean?" When you contemplate this question, you start to realize that the concept of "I" is far from simple. Our sense of who we are is intertwined with what we are thinking, feeling, or experiencing. In the "Who am I?" meditation, we seek to separate the subject ("I") from the object (our experiences).

1 *Sit in a comfortable meditation position. Spend some minutes on a meditation practice you are familiar with, such as a concentration practice or choiceless awareness.*

2 *When your mind is steady, introduce the question "Who am I?" into your mind. Do not try to answer this question in an analytical way, but simply hold it as an inquiring thought.*

3 *You may find it easier to use the question: "Who is breathing?" or "Who is thinking?"*

4 *Do not expect an answer. Over time, your mind may come up with many replies or theories, but there is no intellectual truth that can answer the question "Who am I?"*

5 *At times, you may glimpse an insight that takes you beyond intellectual to what you cannot know. This can be described as consciousness, pure being, or the eternal self (atman, in Hindu philosophy, see page 10). To rest in this consciousness is the ultimate expression of meditation.*

Asking the Question

Self-inquiry is a process that we bring into every moment. As you look at a beautiful view, try asking yourself: "Who is seeing?" Or as you listen to a piece of music, ask yourself: "Who is the hearer?"

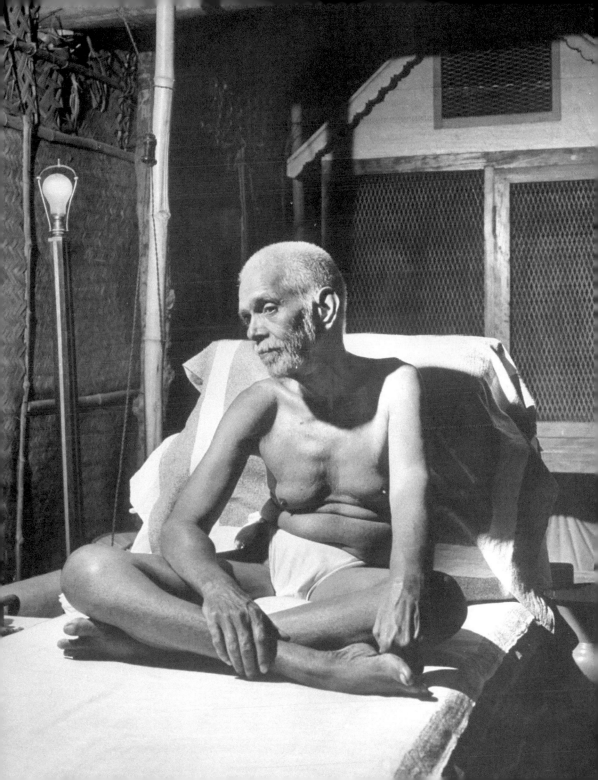

SIX ELEMENTS MEDITATION

This Buddhist practice is a contemplation of the four elements of ancient wisdom—fire, earth, air, water—in conjunction with the two additional "elements" (we might now call them dimensions) of space and consciousness. This meditation can help us gain an insight into the idea

1 *Settle into a comfortable posture, and practice a familiar meditation style, for example, awareness of the breath, to steady your mind.*

Earth

2 *Bring to mind the element of earth. This is everything that is solid and gives shape. Contemplate the solid matter in the body: flesh and skin; muscles and sinews; heart, brain, and other organs.*

3 *Now bring to mind the earth element that is outside the body. This means the floor or chair you are sitting on, the building you are in; hills, trees and cities. Let your mind envisage all these outward aspects of the earth element.*

4 *Consider that the solid earth elements of the body are drawn from the earth elements in the outside world—from the bodies of our parents, from the food we consume. And that the earth elements of our bodies return to the outside world—on a daily basis when we cut nails or hair, or excrete, and conclusively when our bodies become dust. We do not own the earth element; we make use of it and we let it go.*

of impermanence (the idea that all things pass) and interconnectedness (the idea that all things are one) by teaching us that our bodies are not fixed entities, and that they are inextricably interlinked with the world around us.

Water

5 *Contemplate the element of water in the body—saliva, blood, sweat, urine, tears, the fluids in our spine and around our brain.*

6 *Now bring to mind the water element outside the body—in rivers, oceans, and puddles, in faucets, and in the rain. Consider how the water element in the body is replenished by the water elements outside of it—first our mother's milk, then the fluids that we imbibe.*

7 *Water, like earth, is given back—through urination, sweating, crying, and eventually through death. We do not own the water element; we make use of it and we let it go.*

Continued overleaf

Fire

8 *Be aware of the warmth of your body as a manifestation of the fire element. Contemplate the digestive process—which is a kind of burning of the food we eat. Know that this fire in the body is no different to the fire outside—the warmth of the sun, the heat of the oven.*

9 *Just as we take in heat, so, too, do we release it. We radiate heat while we live, and we relinquish it when we die. We do not own the fire element; we make use of it and we let it go.*

Air

10 Now become aware of the element of air in the body—the breath that passes in and out, the oxygen in our blood. Know that this air in the body is no different to the wind or the air we move in.

11 Throughout our lives we take in air and release it. And when we die, we give back a final breath. We do not own the air element; we make use of it and we let it go. The body is in constant flux, taking from the outside world and giving back.

Space and consciousness

12 Notice the spaces in the physical body—the mouth and nostrils, the gaps between fingers and limbs. Note, too, that the body is occupying space. Be aware that the element of space exists inside the body and outside, too. When we die, we surrender the space we occupy. We do not own space; we make use of it and we let it go.

13 Finally, be aware of the element of consciousness. All consciousness is transitory—we host a thought or an emotion, then it disappears. We are not our consciousness, and it is no more fixed or owned than the elements that pass through us. We make use of consciousness, and we let it go.

SKY-GAZING MEDITATION

This practice comes from the Dzogchen tradition of Tibetan Buddhism, which emphasizes that inherent human nature is one of pure awareness. The sky is commonly used as an analogy for awareness in Buddhism, because just as the sky is undisturbed by the clouds that pass over it, so, too, is the spacious mind undisturbed by thoughts or emotions. This sky-gazing meditation offers a way to open our gaze and access our essential nature of open awareness.

1 *Find a high, open area, where you have a clear and uninterrupted view of a wide expanse of the sky, away from the sun.*

2 *Stand in a comfortable meditation pose for some moments. Take long, deep breaths, letting your breath ebb and flow and gently relaxing your body with each out breath.*

3 *Keeping your posture erect, raise your head and look upward, gazing at the sky, so that all you see is sky and nothing more.*

4 *As you breathe out, imagine your breath evaporates into the limitless sky. Breathe out all your worries and thoughts, all the concerns of your narrow self. They are dissipating into the sky.*

5 *As you breathe in, imagine that you are breathing in sky, which dissolves into the skylike awareness that lies within you.*

6 *Keep breathing in and out, letting your mind be as one with the wide open sky.*

7 *At the end of the meditation, slowly lower your head and take a few breaths before moving on.*

Be With What Is

In this—and in all meditations—it is important to avoid trying to engineer some kind of mystical experience. If that is what you are doing, you are no longer in the here and now of your experience. Notice any desire for something to "happen" and let it drop, just as you do any other obstacle or distraction.

Deity Yoga

Deity yoga is part of the tantric tradition and involves invoking a deity through visualization, and also through mantras and chanting. The ultimate aim is to realize that you and the deity are one and the same, as if the deity were a reflection of yourself in a mirror. When you are able to experience this practice completely, the illusion of the deity falls away, but your sense of being an enlightened being remains. In this way, we use the power of the imagination to gain insight into the self—and to cultivate the qualities of this higher being within.

The qualities of the gods

Both Hinduism and Tibetan Buddhism have a pantheon of deities representing particular qualities or characteristics, which can be used for this type of meditation. For example, White Tara, commonly invoked in Tibetan Buddhism, is a mother figure, embodying love and protection. It's important to note that in Tibetan Buddhism a deity is not a god at all, but an enlightened being. So the deity figures are not objects of worship—this is not a form of idolatry. It is truer to think of the deities as archetypes.

Divine role play

Deity yoga is an advanced practice, and is traditionally taught in Tibetan Buddhism only when the meditator has a good understanding of the scriptures and a solid foundation in awareness and concentration practices. However, a simplified form of the practice—such as the one on the following pages—can be an interesting exercise to try, even if you are new to meditation.

Some teachers maintain that deity yoga can be a useful way of working with psychological blockages and issues concerning power or acceptance. In this sense, it is an extension of the role playing commonly used in modern therapeutic settings in order to experiment with new behaviors and experiences.

You do not need to subscribe to any particular belief system in order to do it, because you visualize a deity who is meaningful to you. Alternatively, if you have a wise and compassionate meditation teacher, you can use him or her instead—this is known as guru yoga.

HIGHER BEING MEDITATION

This tantric practice, known as deity yoga or guru yoga, is commonly practiced in yogic meditation and in Tibetan Buddhism, but it can be adapted for any spiritual tradition. It's a way of invoking the supreme qualities of a respected figure or higher being in ourselves—and thereby activating the essential goodness of our inner being.

1 *Relax in a comfortable meditation position, breathing with awareness for some minutes until you feel ready to start.*

2 *With your eyes gently closed, bring to mind an image of a deity or higher power who is meaningful to you. This could be the Buddha, Muhammad, Jesus, Shiva, or—if you prefer—a living teacher or figure you respect and admire.*

3 *Visualize this teacher sitting before you, smiling at you with compassion and wisdom. Understand that you do not have to do anything, or change anything about yourself, to bathe in the warmth of your deity or teacher's gaze.*

4 *As you open up to the warmth and compassion embodied by your deity or teacher, know that these qualities are also within you. Experience these qualities within you as you continue to visualize your deity or teacher before you.*

5 *Have a sense of connection to your deity or teacher. Let your mind merge into that of the guru. Know that you are one and the same, and there is no separation or difference between you.*

6 *Knowing that you have absorbed the qualities of the deity or teacher, let his or her image dissipate. You may want to visualize the image of your deity or teacher becoming transformed into an illuminating source of light.*

7 *Remain sitting, embodying this divine compassion and wisdom, before slowly coming out of the meditation.*

THE CENTERING PRAYER

The centering prayer is a Christian practice first taught in the United States in the 1970s by Trappist monks Thomas Keating, Basil Pennington, and William Meninger. It is based on using a sacred word as a way of opening up to the gift of contemplative prayer, which involves inviting God within. This is different from supplicatory prayer, in which one asks God to intervene and make change happen.

1 *Choose a meaningful word to represent your intention to invite God within. You can ask for God's guidance in selecting an appropriate word—it could be Jesus or Mary, or perhaps a spiritual word, such as hallelujah, amen, shalom, or love, or peace.*

2 *When you have selected your word, you should stay with it throughout the prayer, instead of changing it as if swapping one tool for another that might work better.*

3 *Sit in a comfortable but alert posture, with an upright back. Then close your eyes to reduce sensory distractions, and silently and gently introduce the word into your mind.*

4 *Sit calmly and quietly. You do not need to keep repeating the word, or hold it as a fixed concept in your mind. However, when you notice thoughts, or body sensations, or other distractions, gently direct your attention back to your sacred word.*

5 *Keep in mind that you are not aiming to have a spiritual experience or to receive some special gift of peace. This is a hopeful exercise in communion with God, undertaken in the most propitious conditions—namely, stillness and silence.*

6 *At the end of the allotted time, allow for a short period of adjustment by continuing to sit quietly for two to three minutes.*

A Time for Prayer

It is recommended that you spend at least 20 minutes doing this prayer, twice a day. However, you can start with a shorter time period and build up slowly.

Meditation & Relationships

When we take time out to reflect and meditate, we become more aware in our lives. This awareness can ripple outward to our friends, family, colleagues, and others. So there is no doubt that our solitary practice of meditation can benefit those we have relationships with, and those we encounter in the wider world.

Defusing stress

Countless scientific studies have shown that meditation helps us to handle stress better. Because we tend to vent our stress on those closest to us, there are positive consequences for relationships when we can better handle the anxiety in our lives. For example, we may be less likely to overreact to conflict, more able to step back from it or approach it with patience. We may even be able to find the humor in our day-to-day differences. Greater awareness makes us more able to listen without judgment, and without jumping in.

Domestic harmony

Meditation brings us into the moment, and makes us more aware of the reality of what is going on, including our thoughts and feelings. This can help us to notice when we harbor unrealistic expectations of our partners and loved ones—and thus let them go. Our enhanced awareness may also allow for us to notice when our partner needs something—and thus makes us better able to facilitate his or her happiness. And it can help us to tune into the positives inherent in a healthy relationship, developing and expressing our gratitude for the things our partner or loved ones do for us.

Meditating together

Meditating with your partner or loved ones can be a bonding and fulfilling moment of calm in your day. You may want to make a point of sitting together. Minor issues and difficulties can melt away in the shared silence.

Try making the conscious hugging meditation (see pages 206–7) part of your routine as you say good-bye in the mornings and greet each other in the evenings. Or sit for a few moments and look into the other person's eyes—it can be very powerful.

CONSCIOUS HUGGING MEDITATION

Conscious hugging is a wonderful way to connect with loved ones, to come into the moment, and to enhance our awareness. Hugging also makes us feel good—when we relax into an embrace, it triggers the release of the hormone oxytocin, which promotes bonding and feelings of connecting. One study even found that hugging helps us to deal more effectively with existential concerns, such as the fear of death and the feeling that life is meaningless.

1 *Stand directly opposite your partner or loved one. Take some deep slow breaths, letting your body release tension as you exhale.*

2 *Embrace warmly, with each of you putting your arms around the other in a comfortable way.*

Spiritual Huggers

Hugging meditation is taught at Plum Village in France, the retreat center of the Vietnamese monk and mindfulness teacher Thich Nhat Hanh (see page 17). Hugging is also a practice of the Hindu spiritual leader Mata Amritanandamayi Devi (known as Amma). She gives darshan—literally, "viewings" but often translated as "audiences" or perhaps "blessings"—at which she hugs her followers one by one. She is said to have hugged more than 33 million people and is often referred to as the hugging guru.

3 *Let yourselves relax into the hug. Lean in as you breathe deeply, acknowledging that you are present in this moment—and glad to be here.*

4 *Continue to hold this person, breathing naturally and acknowledging that he or she is also present in this moment— and glad to be here.*

5 *Enjoy the fact that both of you are present in this moment, with nothing to do other than hold each other. Keep the hug going for at least 20 seconds.*

6 *Release the embrace, and thank each other for being here in this moment.*

LISTENING MEDITATION

When we are in conversation, we often become focused on talking. Listening becomes a superficial process—something we do halfheartedly. This can happen particularly to those we are closest to, because we think we know what they are going to say. Here is a way to turn listening into a meditative experience.

1 *Be present. Take a breath and stop doing anything else. Put your cell phone out of sight, turn off the TV or radio. Make a point of focusing exclusively on what is being said.*

2 *Be sense aware. Let your awareness encompass the speaker's face and its expressions, the hand gestures and general quality of the body posture, as well as the words and tone of voice.*

3 *Let go of preparing. If you find yourself thinking about what you want to say, gently bring your attention back to listening.*

4 Notice your reactions. Be aware of emotions, body sensations, judgments, and other thoughts that rise up in you while you are listening. Can you make space for them to be present without letting them direct your responses or distract you from listening?

5 Make space. If an emotion is strong, notice where you feel it in the body and take some slower, deeper breaths. Try to examine it with a sense of interest as it shifts and changes.

6 Pause before speaking. Notice the temptation to interrupt or change the subject, and try to let it go. When you want to respond, take a breath before speaking. Let go of the need to come up with a solution or answer if you need time to reflect.

Children & Meditation

Teaching children about meditation can help to equip them for handling everyday stress. It can improve their mental and emotional well-being, which is why it is increasingly taught in schools. One study by researchers at the University of British Columbia found that a program incorporating mindfulness helped increase emotional control and empathy in children, while a Korean study found that teaching meditation helped ease social anxiety, aggression, and depression in school pupils.

Sharing your practice

Children tend to be interested in what their parents do—especially when young—and learn by copying their behavior. So your children are more likely to take to meditation if they see you doing it. Try letting your children sit quietly near you while you sit. Depending on their age, it can be a good idea to provide activities such as coloring or jigsaw puzzles, so they can play without disturbing you. But you may find that they will naturally sit beside you.

You can suggest a regular meditation time for the whole family, perhaps as a daily habit or a weekly one. Make sure that the space is suitable and that everyone has their own seat or cushion. It can be nice to make time for meditation in the morning, to set the tone for a calm day, but an afternoon or evening sit may better suit your family's routine (see pages 214–15 for some guidelines).

Intention over results

Children may want to sit on some days and not on others. Or they may prefer quiet walking meditation or mini mindfulness exercises instead of more formal practices. Notice if you have a desire for your children to have a particular reaction or experience—such as becoming calmer or staying absolutely still—when you practice meditation with them. If your child is not interested in meditation at this time, remember that having a parent who is practicing meditation can benefit children in indirect ways.

MEDITATION FOR PARENTS

It's not easy to meditate when you have children. The standard advice may be to get up earlier for practice, but there are a number of reasons why this is not possible for many parents. Here are some ways to meditate when parenting militates against it.

1 *Try mindful playing. Instead of conjuring up time to sit, make time with your children a form of mindfulness practice. Get down on the floor and play with them, or snuggle up and read, bringing all your attention and awareness to each moment.*

2 *Look ahead. Visualize the future day when nobody wakes you at dawn, and there are no toys scattered on the living room floor. Recognize that this chaotic time of your life is temporary. And remember that every day contains moments to treasure.*

3 *Choose an activity. If meditation feels like another thing to fit in, let it go. Think of a task that you do each day—filling the dishwasher, sweeping the kitchen floor—and make a point of doing this task with mindful attention.*

4 *Notice the struggle. Check in regularly to assess how your mind and body is (see pages 64–67). If you notice tension, take a deep breath and try to let this go. Notice any sense of battling or endurance. Is it necessary at this moment?*

5 *Hear your inner voice. Most people find that parenting is more stressful than they expected, and it can be sad to find yourself shouting or talking to your child in a harsh way. Notice the temptation to berate yourself for this; be kind to yourself. Parenting, like meditation, means taking a breath and starting over again.*

6 *Put your cell phone away. A few moments talking to friends on social media can seem like a necessary escape. But all the same, make a point of putting your cell phone to one side while you are with your children and at mealtimes.*

MICROMEDITATIONS FOR CHILDREN It's important to keep

children's sessions short and enjoyable. Use a timer and at first set it to one or two minutes. Here are some easy meditations to share with your children. If you prefer, you can adapt some of the simpler exercises from this book.

Breathe with a bear

Focusing on the breath can be a useful way to teach awareness— and it gives children a handy strategy for learning relaxation, too. Try to get your children to practice belly breathing while lying down and show them how their belly moves. You can place a soft toy on their belly so they can see the actions of the breath more easily.

Breathe along your hand

Another way of working with the breath is to use the finger of one hand to trace the rhythm of the breath along the outline

of the other fingers and thumb. Breathe in and gently run your right index finger along the outside of the pinkie finger on the other hand. Pause at the top, then breathe out

and run it along the inside of the pinkie finger, pause at the base, then breathe in and run it up the outside of the ring finger and so on.

Send good wishes

The loving-kindness meditation can also be enjoyable for children. Get them to sit comfortably and then use the instructions on pages 138–41 to guide them through the stages. Some children like to imagine the good wishes that they are sending as a favorite color.

Your safe place

Get your children to lie down comfortably and then take them on an imaginary walk through a beautiful forest, or try reading out the beach meditation on pages 150–51. This form of meditation can be particularly good at bedtime.

GLOSSARY

Bodhisattva Sanskrit term used in Mahayana Buddhism for a person who is able to reach nirvana but delays doing so for the sake of others.

Brahma The supreme god in Hinduism.

Chakra Energy center in the body, according to yogic philosophy; the seven main chakras lie along the midline of the body, from the base of the spine to the crown of the head. The word "chakra" comes from the Sanskrit word for "wheel."

Chi Energy or life force; a concept used in Taoism and Chinese medicine.

Choiceless/open awareness Form of meditation in which there is no specific object, but one attends to whatever is occurring in the present moment.

Dantian The three main energy centers of the body, according to Taoist philosophy. Can be likened to the chakras used in yogic philosophy.

Dharma Teachings of the Buddha. The term is also used in Sikhism and Hinduism to suggest "natural law."

Dzogchen Meaning "great perfection" or "great completeness," this is a tradition of teachings in Tibetan Buddhism that is intended to help one realize the true nature of the mind.

Kundalini Form of energy located at the base of the spine, according to yogic philosophy.

Mahayana One of two major traditions in Buddhism; the other is Theravada. Mahayana literally means the "great vehicle" in Sanskrit.

Mala String of beads used as an aid to meditation in Buddhism, Hinduism, and Sikhism.

Mandala Buddhist spiritual image that symbolizes the universe and is used as an aid to meditation. Sand mandalas are created with colored sands—a process that can take many days—and then destroyed as a metaphor for the impermanent nature of life.

Mantra Sacred sound, word, or short phrase that is repeated silently or out loud as a form of meditation. See also "Om."

Meridian Energy pathways through the body, according to Taoism and Chinese medicine.

Metta Unconditional positive regard, or loving-kindness. The practice of metta (or metta bhavana) is a Buddhist meditation.

Mindfulness Term used for paying attention to the present moment with full awareness.

Moksha The highest form of consciousness in Hinduism and Jainism, and the moment when one becomes released from the shackles of human existence. It is closely related to the concept of nirvana in Buddhism.

Monkey mind Term used by Buddhists for a mind that leaps from one thought to another.

Nadi Energy pathways in the body, according to yogic philosophy. The central nadi is the sushumna, which links the base chakra to the crown chakra.

Neidan Used in Taoism, this term means "inner alchemy"

and is the name used for meditative practices that aim to promote good mental, physical, and spiritual health—and ultimately to attain spiritual enlightenment.

Nirvana Enlightenment, or the highest state of consciousness (in Buddhism).

Niyama Ethical guideline, according to yogic philosophy. See also yama.

Om Spiritual sound and the most sacred mantra used in yogic and Buddhist practice.

Samatha Practice to calm the mind by focusing on a particular object, such as the breath. It is used in both yogic and Buddhist practice.

Seva The concept of service, used in Hinduism.

Singing bowl Tibetan bowl made from brass, which makes a harmonic sound when struck or if a mallet is run over the rim.

Soham The sound of the breath, according to yogic philosophy; a spiritual mantra.

Soji A period of time in which one carries out chores mindfully in a Zen monastery or nunnery.

Tantra Spiritual philosophy, derived from Hinduism and used in some Buddhist traditions. Tantric practices use the power of the senses to achieve spiritual understanding; the Sanskrit term can be translated as "weaving together."

Tao Literally meaning "the way," a term is used to denote the natural order of the universe in which all things change, and the spiritual pathway in which one lives in harmony with this.

Theravada One of two major traditions of Buddhism. It adheres to the teachings of the Buddha as outlined in the Pali scriptures. It literally means "doctrine of the elders" but is sometimes called "the lesser vessel" (cf. "the greater vessel" of Mahayan Buddhism).

Tonglen Tibetan Buddhist "giving-and-taking" meditation in which one imagines taking in the suffering of others and sending out healing.

Trataka Yogic practice in which one gazes on an object.

Vajrayana The tantric tradition of Buddhism, which is notably practiced in Tibet.

Vedas Collection of Hindu texts, probably written between 1500 and 700 BCE.

Vipassana A key Buddhist practice, defined as "insight into how things really are." It is the basis of modern mindfulness meditation.

Yama Ethical guideline to how not to behave, used in Hinduism. See also niyama.

Yantra Spiritual painting used as an aid to meditation in Hinduism. A yantra is a geometric pattern using concentric shapes, similar to a Buddhist mandala.

Yoga nada Term meaning "union through sound," used for meditations that employ sound for spiritual realization.

Zen School of Buddhism that developed in Japan. Part of the Mahayana tradition.

FURTHER READING

Chia, Mantak. *Healing Light of the Tao: Foundational Practices to Awaken Chi Energy.*
Destiny Books, 2008.

Chia, Mantak. *The Inner Smile: Increasing Chi through the Cultivation of Joy.*
Destiny Books, 2008.

Dalai Lama, The. *Stages of Meditation: Training the Mind for Wisdom.*
Rider, 2003.

Gyatso, Geshe Kelsang. *The New Meditation Handbook.*
Tharpa Publications, 2013.

Kabat-Zinn, Jon. *Wherever You Go, There You Are: Mindfulness Meditation for Everyday Life.*
Piatkus, 2004.

Kornfield, Jack and Joseph Goldstein. *Seeking the Heart of Wisdom: The Path of Insight Meditation.*
Shambala Publications, 2001.

Nhat Hanh, Thich. *The Miracle of Mindfulness: The Classic Guide to Meditation by the World's Most Revered Master.*
Rider, 2008.

Rinpoche, Sogyal. *Tibetan Book of Living and Dying.*
Rider, 2008.

Salzberg, Sharon. *Lovingkindness: The Revolutionary Art of Happiness.*
Shambala Publications, 2002.

Suzuki, Shunryu. *Zen Mind, Beginner's Mind.*
Shambala, 2011.

Titmuss, Christopher. *An Awakened Life.*
Rider, 2014.

USEFUL ADDRESSES & WEB SITES

ADDRESSES

United States

Insight Meditation Society
1230 Pleasant St.
Barre
MA 01005
www.dharma.org

Namgyal Monastery Institute of Buddhist Studies
PO Box 127
Ithaca
NY 14850
www.namgyal.org

Spirit Rock
5000 Sir Francis Drake Blvd.
Woodacre
CA 94973
www.spiritrock.org

Zenshuji Soto Mission
123 S Hewitt St.
Los Angeles
CA 90012
www.zenshuji.org/

UK

Gaia House
West Ogwell
Newton Abbot
Devon TQ12 6EW
www.gaiahouse.org

International Zen Assocation
Bristol Zen Dojo
91/93 Gloucester Road
Bristol
BS7 8AT
www.izauk.org

The Buddhist Society
58 Eccleston Square
London
SW1V 1PH
www.thebuddhistsociety.org

The Shambala Centre
27 Belmont Close
London
SW4 6AY
www.shambala.org.uk

FRANCE

Plum Village Mindfulness Practice Centre
Communauté Bouddhique Zen
Village des Pruniers
Meyrac 47120
Loubes-Bernac
www.plumvillage.org

WEB SITES

www.buddhanet.org

www.dharmaseed.org
For free Western Buddhist Vipassana Teachings

www.universal-tao.com
The website for Mantak Chia and his Taoist teachings

Association for Insight Meditation
www.aimwell.org

www.bluecliffmonastery.org/monastic-practice-centers

INDEX

ACKNOWLEDGMENTS

With thanks to Christopher Titmuss and Sharda Rogell, who opened my mind and heart to insight meditation and to metta. The benefits really did keep coming in the weeks, months, and years after Bodh Gaya.

PICTURE ACKNOWLEDGMENTS

Every effort has been made to trace copyright holders and obtain permission. The publishers apologize for any omissions and would be pleased to make any necessary changes at subsequent printings.

Alamy/Dinodia Photos / Alamy Stock Photo: 183. **Archives Office of Tasmania**/ 88–89. **Dead Media Archive**/ 88–89. **Getty**/ Eliot Elisofon / Contributor: 191; Suzanne Opton / Contributor: 126. **Louis Mackay**/ Eliot Elisofon / Contributor: 126. **Louis Mackay**/ 35. **Shutterstock**/ 2happy: 64–65; 4Max: 17; Valentin Agapov: 162–63; Nenad Aksic: 110; Pilar Alcaro: 108–9; Ozerov Alexander: 53; Alina G: 172–73; All About Space: 72T; Amovitania: 120–21; andreiuc88: 90–91; Galyna Andrushko: 162–63; anetta: 172–73; Subbotina Anna: 128–29; antshev: 108–9; aquariagirl1970: 146–47; ArtMari: 170–71; artnana: 152–53; arvitalyaa: 156–57; autovector: 74–75; Ann Baldwin: 144; Brady Barrineau: 9; basel101658: 82–83; Be Good: 73; bikeriderlondon: 192; Billion Photos: 60–61; BLFootage: 25; Blueguy: 150–51; Boonsom: 8; Brzostowska: 156–57; Suttha Burawonk: 64–65; byvalet: 142–43; Anatoliy Cherkas: 51; chippix: 138–39; Chombosan: 66–67; CKP1001: 58–59; critterbiz: 88–89; William Cushman: 11; Ditty_about_summer: 155; djgis: 195; donatas1205: 160-161; Drakuliren: 152–53; Drop of Light: 108–9; Olga Drozdova: 152–53; Misha Dudov: 142–43; echo3005: 140–41; elfinadesign: 128–29; Ensuper: 74–75; Es75: 70–71; ESBuka: 93; Evannovostro: 181; Everett Collection: 138–39, 146–47, 150–51, 152–53; Evgenia L: 115; Dory F: 13B; faestock: 118–19; Yossawat fangseing: 76–77; Feaspb: 132–33; Hugo Felix: 107; file404: 128–29; frankie's: 150–51; G.roman: 170–71; Gajus: 184–85; Genova: 80–81; Gilmanshin: 54–55; GlebStock: 197; Alex Gontar: 128–29; Kamil Hajek: 158–59; Happy Together: 15B; Shawn Hempel: 142–43; henrik1978: 90–91; Patricia Hofmeester: 120–21; Hot Property: 170–71; Hundley Photography: 82–83; hybridtechno: 76–77; Daniela Illing: 76–77; ImagePost: 64–65; Tischenko Irina: 142–43; irin-k: 90–91; isarescheewin: 99; iwoma: 54–55; ixpert: 150–51; Jag_cz: 33, 166–67; uttawee Jai: 132–33; jeenamoolstudio: 60–61; jocic: 120–21; Kamira: 54–55; Karuka: 172–73; Anastasiia Kazakova: 66–67; Robert Kneschke: 205; KonstantinChristian: 137; Patryk Kosmider: 118–19; Kovaleva_Ka: 146–47; Kozlik: 56–57; kpboonjit: 172–73; Lev Kropotov: 138–39; KUCO: 82–83; Tamara Kulikova: 60–61, 82–83; kuruneko: 165; Neil Lang: 162–63; William Langeveld: 80–81; laverock: 132–33; Lifestyle_Studio: 178–79; LiliGraphie: 152–53; littleny: 108–9; tommaso lizzul: 76–77; Lolostock: 103; luckyraccoon: 127; lynea: 74-75; Richard Lyons: 21; Dariush M: 14T; Ihnatovich Maryia: 74–75; Marzolino: 76–77; Masson: 80–81; MASTER PHOTO 2017: 64–65; MaxyM: 64–65; Mclek: 52T; Dudarev Mikhail: 95; mikser45: 146–47; MJTH: 19; Monkey Business Images: 135; Giorgio Morara: 60–61; Morphart Creation: 54–55, 66–67, 150–51, 160–61; most popular: 160–61; MRAORAOR: 64–65; Resul Muslu: 166–67; mything: 160–61; nd3000: 187; Roman Nerud: 138–39, 158–59, 176–77; Nicvandum: 118–19; Mahesh Patil: 10; Nixx Photography: 142–43; Nobeastsofierce: 128–29; Hein Nouwens: 140–41, 176–77; SUMITH NUNKHAM: 201; paintings: 53; palidachan: 142–43; Petar Paunchev: 111; petefrone: 166–67; Vadim Petrakov: 132–33; PHOTOCREO Michal Bednarek: 145; Photographee. eu: 108–9; PhotoMediaGroup: 66–67; Piyapongd140: 199; PlanilAstro: 88–89; PlusONE: 90–91; Progressfoto: 170–71; Purino: 123; Pushish Images: 13T; R3BV: 150–51; Akhil Raj R B: 79; Rarana: 84–85; Rawpixel.com: 22–23, 26–27; rdonar: 90–91; Martial Red: 128–29; RemarkEliza: 54–55; Alf Ribeiro: 108-109; romualdi: 146–47; s-ts: 66–67; SanchaiRat: 30–31; schankz: 172–73; BorisShevchuk: 80–81; Egon Schiele: 90–91; David M. Schrader: 146–47; science photo: 118–19; sebra: 120–21; Elzbieta Sekowska: 76–77, 132–33, 140–41, 160–61, 166–67; Natalia Sheinkin: 56–57; Maksim Shmeljov: 64–65; Stieber: 172–73; Artem Stepanov: 150–51; Shelly Still: 158–59; StockLite: 106; stockpackshot: 74–75; Kuttelvaserova Stuchelova: 152–53; -strizh-: 138–39; Nopporn Subyen: 108–09; SunisaStock: 176–77; Ferenc Szelepcsenyi: 189; takayuki: 146–47; Nopkamon Tanayakorn: 108–9; Teia: 76–77; TJmedia: 70–71; TongRo Images Inc: 156–57; Triff: 88–89; SAYAM TRIRATTANAPAIBOON: 64–65; Andy Troy: 158–59; Neo Tribbiani: 70–71; Tuzemka: 130–31; Luna Vandoorne: 203; Martins Vanags: 90–91; varuna: 193; VectorShow: 152–53; Victorian Traditions: 162–63; wavebreakmedia: 128–29, 211; Liubou Yasiukovich: 74–75; yelantsevv: 194; Y Photo Studio: 102; Yuii: 74–75; yuratosno3: 154; Anton Zabielskyi: 56–57; Olga Zelenkova: 169; Liu zishan: 128–29, 172–73. **The Graphics Fairy**/ 84–85. **Vintage Image Photos**/ 88–89. **Wikimedia Commons**/ mettabebe: 16B.